THE BUSINESS MODEL

HOW TO DEVELOP NEW PRODUCTS, CREATE MARKET VALUE AND MAKE THE COMPETITION IRRELEVANT

ALEXANDER CHERNEV

Kellogg School of Management

Northwestern University

The Business Model: How to Develop New Products,
Create Market Value and Make the Competition Irrelevant

March 2017

ISBN: 978-1-936572-45-8

Published by Cerebellum Press, Inc., USA

CONTENTS

ABOUT THE AUTHOR

Alexander Chernev is a professor of marketing at the Kellogg School of Management, Northwestern University. He holds a PhD in psychology from Sofia University and a PhD in business administration from Duke University.

Dr. Chernev has written numerous articles focused on business strategy, brand management, consumer behavior, and market planning. His research has been published in the leading marketing journals and has been frequently quoted in the business and popular press, including *The Wall Street Journal*, *Financial Times*, *The New York Times*, *The Washington Post*, *Harvard Business Review*, *Scientific American*, *Associated Press*, *Forbes*, and *Business Week*. He was ranked among the top ten most prolific scholars in the leading marketing journals by the *Journal of Marketing* and among the top five marketing faculty in the area of consumer behavior by a global survey of marketing faculty published by the *Journal of Marketing Education*.

Dr. Chernev's books—*Strategic Marketing Management*, *Strategic Brand Management*, *The Marketing Plan Handbook*, and *The Business Model: How to Develop New Products, Create Market Value, and Make the Competition Irrelevant*—have been translated into multiple languages and are used in top business schools around the world. He serves as an area editor for the *Journal of Marketing* and is on the editorial boards of leading research journals, including the *Journal of Marketing Research*, *Journal of Consumer Research*, *Journal of Consumer Psychology*, *Journal of the Academy of Marketing Science*, and *Journal of Marketing Behavior*.

Dr. Chernev teaches marketing strategy, brand management, and behavioral decision theory in MBA, PhD, and executive education programs at the Kellogg School of Management. He has also taught in executive programs at INSEAD in France and Singapore, at IMD in Switzerland, and at Hong Kong University of Science and Technology. He has received numerous awards, including the Core Course Teaching Award, Faculty Impact Award, and the Top Professor Award from the Kellogg Executive MBA Program, which he has received nine times.

In addition to research and teaching, Dr. Chernev is an Academic Trustee of the *Marketing Science Institute* and advises companies around the world on issues of marketing strategy, brand management, consumer behavior, pricing, strategic planning, and new product development. He has worked with Fortune 500 companies on ways to reinvent their business models, develop new products, and gain competitive advantage. He has helped multiple startups uncover market opportunities, discover new business models, and craft market strategies.

ACKNOWLEDGMENTS

This book has benefited from the wisdom of many of my current and former colleagues at the Kellogg School of Management at Northwestern University. I am also indebted to students in the MBA and Executive MBA programs that I have taught at the Kellogg School of Management, INSEAD, and Hong Kong Institute of Science and Technology, who have motivated me to write this book and helped shape its content. I would also like to thank Alejandro Arteaga, Bogomil Balkansky, Aaron Brough, Carter Cast, Jerome Deveix, Ryan Hamilton, and Matt Huebner for their valuable comments. I am also grateful to Joanne Freeman for editing this book with a very keen and helpful eye.

PREFACE

It started with a simple idea: Most people hate grocery shopping. Getting to the store and searching for the desired items can be an effortful and time-consuming task. Grocery stores offer a limited assortment of items, and consumers might end up going to a store only to find that what they are looking for is not in stock. And even if they find the desired items, they might have to trade off quality and price, with high-quality produce priced at a substantial premium.

Now imagine a company that offers consumers the convenience of same-day home delivery within a customer-selected 30-minute window; a broad selection of high-quality fresh foods including produce, hand-cut meats, fresh fish and live lobsters, non-perishable grocery items, chef-prepared meals, and fine wines; and prices that are at or below everyday supermarket prices, with no membership or service fees, and free delivery for orders over $50.

Sound exciting? It did — to a number of top-notch venture capital investors including Sequoia Capital, Benchmark Capital, Softbank, Yahoo!, and Goldman Sachs. The new enterprise raised close to $800 million in venture funding and from its oversubscribed IPO. The head of the management firm Andersen Consulting (now Accenture) resigned to join the company. What could go wrong? Everything…

Once touted as one of the top e-commerce startups, the new venture burned through hundreds of millions of dollars and closed shop 18 months after going public. The company's stock plummeted from $30 to six cents within a few months, erasing over a billion dollars of market capitalization. It became known as the largest flop of the dot-com bubble. As you might have guessed, we are talking about Webvan.

So, what went wrong?

Some blame it on consumers' inertia. Grocery shopping, although unpleasant, was not a burning problem that consumers were in a rush to solve. After all, Webvan was not the only game in town. The traditional brick-and-mortar stores frequented by consumers for many years had not disappeared overnight. Driven by the power of habit, consumers were slow to give Webvan a try.

Others argued that Webvan targeted the wrong customers and should have limited its service to densely populated areas rather than across entire metro areas. As a result of Webvan's attempt to offer broad service coverage, delivery trucks were underutilized, making long delivery trips to deliver only a few orders.

Still others believed that in an attempt to appeal to a wide customer base, Webvan carried an overly broad assortment of items that dramatically increased its costs. In addition, home delivery was both costly and time-consuming, adding to Webvan's ballooning cost structure. It was also suggested that Webvan encountered a number of logistical issues with the automation of its warehouses and delivery scheduling.

The collapse of Webvan was also attributed to the fact that the competition — the network of brick-and-mortar retailers, suppliers, processors, wholesalers, and distributors — might not have been as inefficient as Webvan assumed. That the Webvan executive team had very limited experience in the retail grocery field was yet another contributing factor to its downfall.

It was also suggested that Webvan failed because it scaled up too fast. Rather than streamlining operations in its primary market—San Francisco—prior to expanding to other cities, Webvan invested $1 billion to build a number of state-of-the-art order fulfillment centers, each over $30 million, while also aggressively investing in van fleets. Yet, Webvan's customer base and margins were not large enough to support its overly ambitious goal of expanding into 26 markets in two years. The $1.2 billion acquisition of chief rival HomeGrocer.com contributed to depleting the company's already scarce resources.

With so many different contributing factors, one might ask: What was the primary cause of Webvan's implosion?

All the above reasons can be boiled down to a single overarching cause: Webvan did not have a sound *business model* that clearly outlined how the company would create value for its customers and capture value for its shareholders. Instead, Webvan invested close to a billion dollars in an idea that was not backed up by a viable business model; it focused on a large-scale execution without an adequate understanding of how the company would create market value.

Now consider AmazonFresh, Amazon's online grocery shopping service launched in 2007, six years after the demise of Webvan. Amazon avoided many of Webvan's mistakes and was able to successfully grow its market footprint. Even though both companies operated in the same industry—online grocery retail—their business models varied on several dimensions.

First, the two companies differed in their choice of target customers. Unlike Webvan, which was focused on growth at any cost, Amazon was much more strategic in choosing its target customers. Rather than initially launching its services in entire metropolitan areas, Amazon focused only on areas with a high concentration of potential customers. This selective approach enabled Amazon to build an effective and cost-efficient distribution system.

The second important difference between Webvan and Amazon was pricing. While both companies offered free delivery on orders over $50, Amazon also required a $299 membership to use its grocery service. This pricing structure enabled Amazon to ensure that its grocery service would create value not only for its customers but also for the company.

Another differentiating factor was the rate at which the two companies grew their businesses. For Webvan, it was all about the speed of growth; for Amazon it was about getting the business model right. Webvan committed to large capital expenditures before thoroughly testing its core concept, rapidly scaling up its operations before achieving success in its primary market. In contrast, Amazon was painstakingly validating its concept by starting with an invitation-only beta test at a single location on Mercer Island near Seattle. A year later, it expanded its operations to the city of Seattle where the company was headquartered. It was several years before it started gradually expanding to the densely populated areas of cities that included Los Angeles, San Francisco, San Diego, Philadelphia, Boston, and London.

Furthermore, while Webvan's business was based on the premise if you build it, they will come, Amazon was much more focused on what exactly needed to be built. Webvan failed to develop a clear understanding of the needs and behavior of its target customers, underestimated the competition from traditional retailers, and misidentified the opportunities and threats associated with the retail grocery industry. In contrast, Amazon invested significant resources—time, money, and effort—in developing and validating its business model before scaling it up. Amazon's approach, often referred to as validated learning, is based on the idea that a viable business model requires a thorough understanding of the market—what customer needs are, how customers are likely to behave, and what assets and competencies a company must have to create value in this market.

Having a viable business model meant the difference between success and failure for these two ventures. And even though having a viable business model does not guarantee success, not having one is a precursor to a market fiasco—as it was for Webvan.

Many managers, while taking credit for business successes, tend to blame failures on a variety of external factors, including economic conditions, the regulatory environment, and technological developments. Although these factors can contribute to the success or failure of an offering, the key reason that products and companies fail is that they lack a viable business model that outlines how they will create value for their customers and collaborators, and capture value for their stakeholders. This is what this book is all about—creating market value. It lays out the key aspects of developing a business model that helps ensure sustainable value for customers, the company, and its collaborators.

The Business Model offers a systematic approach to identifying market opportunities and developing breakthrough business models. It outlines the key principles of business model generation, presents a value-based framework for developing viable new offerings, and provides a set of practical tools for creating a meaningful value proposition that drives market success.

The book starts out by outlining the key principles inherent in building a business model and highlights the pivotal role that business models play in both startups and established enterprises. It then introduces a value-centric framework for developing a viable business model and creating a market value map. Following the discussion of the structure of business models, the book outlines an approach to business model generation based on the idea of validated learning and offers a set of practical tools that can facilitate business model development. The book concludes with examples of business models of five breakthrough startups that reached a valuation of $1 billion or higher within five years of their launch.

The business model framework outlined in this book applies to a wide range of companies—startups and established enterprises, consumer-packaged-goods companies and business-to-business enterprises, high-tech and low-tech ventures, online and brick-and-mortar entities, product manufacturers and value-added service providers, nonprofit organizations and profit-driven companies.

Practical, actionable, and succinct, *The Business Model* is the essential reference and how-to guide for everyone seeking to achieve market success: from entrepreneurs to experienced managers, from senior executives to product designers, from those creating new market offerings to those improving on existing ones. This book is for those passionate about building great products that create market value and disrupt industries.

1

THE BUSINESS MODEL
OF AN ENTERPRISE

THE BUSINESS MODEL AS A ROADMAP FOR CREATING MARKET VALUE

It is possible to fail in many ways,
while to succeed is possible only in one way.
— Aristotle, Greek philosopher

The development of new products is the engine that fuels the business enterprise. New product success is often attributed to intuition. Indeed, some products that stem from intuition do make it big. Yet many others crash and burn. The reason is that intuition is only one aspect of new product development. The other key ingredient of success is having a systematic approach to creating market value. This systematic approach is the business model of an enterprise.

The Business Model

Imagine you are a manager in charge of a new offering. Like many other managers in a similar situation, you are faced with a number of business decisions. Some of these decisions concern the specifics of the offering — a product or service — that is being readied for market launch. For example:

What features should the new product include?

What services should the company offer?

How should the offering be branded?

At what price should it be offered?

What, if any, sales promotions should it involve?

How will potential customers know about the offering?

How will the offering be delivered to these customers?

Other questions are more general and focus on the market in which this offering will compete and the value it aims to create in that market:

Who are the customers for whom the company should develop an offering?

Why would these customers buy this offering?

What other offerings are available to these customers?

What resources must the company have to create an offering that fulfills this customer need?

Whom should the company partner with?

How will new technologies influence the ways in which the company creates value for its customers?

How will economic conditions and government regulations influence the company's ability to create a successful market offering?

Overwhelmed by the complexity of some of these questions and by the sheer number of issues to be addressed, many managers tend to ignore such questions, hoping that the answers will emerge naturally over time. They rarely do.

Most new products fail because managers neglect to consider a number of the relevant issues and address them in a way that will result in a successful offering. What many failed products are missing is a sound *business model* that clearly delineates how the company's offering will create value in its chosen market.

The business model outlines the ways in which an enterprise creates market value

The business model is the master plan that charts the way in which a company can reach its goals. It streamlines the process by which a company identifies its target market, defines its value proposition in this market, and develops an offering that creates value for its target customers, its collaborators, and its stakeholders. Having a clearly articulated, logical, and sustainable business model is a prerequisite for any enterprise, be it a startup or an established company.

The Business Model of a Startup

Generally speaking, a startup is an organization in the early stages of its operation. Recently, the term *startup* has acquired a narrower meaning that is inextricably linked to the development of new-to-the-world products, the creation of innovative business models, and a focus on rapid and scalable business growth.[1] In this context, a startup is an organization in an early stage of its operation that has been formed to develop a new offering.

The development of a new offering is the defining characteristic of a startup. New product development inevitably involves a level of uncertainty about the market and the technological viability of the offering. New product development also involves generating a business model that delineates the ways in which the offering creates value for the company, its customers, and its collaborators.

Although most startups begin as small ventures, not every small venture is a startup. A small family-owned restaurant, a mom-and-pop retail store, and a small construction company that operate the same way as most other companies in their industry would not be considered startups because they are not set up to develop a new offering.

Not all startups are high-tech. Even though most highly visible startups are in the high-tech industry, this is caused by market opportunities created by the rapid development of technology rather than the fact that startups are the province of the high-tech industry. A beef jerky company developing a new product and creating a new market for this product is as much a startup as a high-tech company developing a new social media app.

Startups vary in the degree of novelty of their business models. Some aim to develop simpler, more effective, and less expensive versions of existing products. Others aim to design new-to-the-world products that previously did not exist in the market. Yet, others aim to develop disruptive business models to displace current business models.

4

Despite their differences, startups share a number of common features. Specifically, most startups are characterized by three key attributes: *uncertainty, flexibility*, and *limited resources*.

- **Uncertainty.** Startups develop new business models in a high-uncertainty environment. This uncertainty spans domains and includes uncertainty about the market, uncertainty about the acceptance of the offering being created, uncertainty about the best organizational structure for the team managing the offering, and uncertainty about the processes involved in creating, promoting, and distributing the new offering. This uncertainty leads to two general types of risk: *technological risk*, which reflects the uncertainty about the technological feasibility of the offering (*can it actually be made?*) and *market risk*, which reflects the market reaction to the new offering, including offering attractiveness (*will customers find the offering attractive?*) and offering viability (*will it create value for the company?*).

- **Flexibility.** A startup is able to make dramatic changes in virtually all aspects of its business model, including the choice of a market in which to operate, the design of the offering, the organizational structure of the company, and the processes involved in designing the offering. Unlike established companies—whose legacy organizational structure, processes, and timelines can make it difficult to depart from their existing way of doing business—startups have greater *degrees of freedom* in tailoring their business model to the current market conditions. As a result, startups tend to be more capable of rapidly identifying new market trends, more likely to respond to these trends by developing new offerings, and more willing to pivot the current business model to better align it with the identified market opportunity.

- **Limited resources.** Another feature most startups have in common is the limited resources they have to develop and implement their business models. These resources are not restricted to the available capital but also involve a wide array of assets—facilities, materials, people, know-how, brands, and access to communication and distribution channels—that are crucial to the development of a successful market offering. As a result, startups are often at a disadvantage compared to incumbent companies with ready access to many of these resources, giving them a leg up on companies seeking to enter their markets.

To build on their strengths and overcome their limitations, startups must be strategic in identifying the right market opportunities, targeting markets that are aligned with their core competencies and assets, and designing offerings that create value both for the company and its customers. To this end, a startup must adopt a systematic approach to new product development and clearly articulate how its offerings will create and capture market value. Thus, the success of a startup hinges on its ability to generate a viable business model.

The Business Model of an Established Enterprise

The mantra of many startup evangelists is that only startups need a business model, whereas established companies do not. Despite the popularity of this view, it is incorrect. To succeed, both startups and established companies need a viable business model. The difference is that startups *must* create a new business model. In contrast, incumbent enterprises already have a business model and are not forced to create a new one. The fact that established companies already have a business model, however, often makes them complacent and oblivious to the need to constantly revisit, and, when necessary, reinvent, their existing business model.

No company can survive without revamping its business model to successfully compete with the constantly changing market environment and with startups seeking to disrupt its business. Companies like Borders, Circuit City, and Blockbuster had to close their doors because they failed to revisit and reinvent the way they were doing business in the face of emerging technologies that gave birth to startups like Amazon.com and Netflix.

Even though startups and established companies rely on business models that have the same structure, follow the same principles, and serve the same functions, they might vary in their approach to business model development. The differences in the way startups and established enterprises develop their business models often stem from their relative advantages and disadvantages.

Established companies have a number of common characteristics that give them an advantage over startups when it comes to developing new offerings: _knowledge_, _experience_, and _resources_.

- **Knowledge.** Because they are familiar with the industry in which they operate and with the underlying technological and business processes used to develop their products and services, established companies often face less uncertainty when developing new offerings. This includes less uncertainty about the technological feasibility of the offering, customer preferences, and the economics of creating a viable offering.

- **Experience.** Established companies often benefit from having the organizational structure and business and technological processes already in place to manage the development of new products. This enables established companies to be more effective and cost efficient in designing and managing their offerings.

- **Resources.** Established companies tend to have greater resources to invest in developing new offerings. Indeed, because they already have existing offerings that generate revenue, these companies can channel some of this revenue into new product development. The ready availability of resources can also relieve some of the pressure on the new offering to create revenue and allow a longer time horizon for the market success of the offering.

Despite their advantages, established companies have two important drawbacks when developing new products: _inertia_ and _legacy constraints_.

- **Inertia.** In the words of the architect of the theory of disruptive innovation, Clayton Christensen, a key challenge facing established companies is the tendency to focus on customers' current needs, neglecting to develop new offerings that will fulfill their future needs. As a result, established companies often fail to take advantage of market trends until their business models have been disrupted and displaced by more agile and forward-looking startups. The great hockey player Wayne Gretzky is often quoted as saying: _I skate to where the puck is going to be, not where it has been_. The problem for many established enterprises is that they end up playing catch-up, guided by business models that reflect the past, not the future.

- **Legacy constraints**. Another drawback of established enterprises is the relatively limited degrees of freedom their product development teams have because of legacy constraints. Whereas a startup can pivot and change its strategic direction relatively easily, established companies face greater constraints on changing strategic direction that are imposed by their existing resources, organization, and processes. As a result, established companies, over time, tend to become less agile in identifying market opportunities and developing new offerings to address these opportunities.

To overcome these limitations and succeed in developing successful market offerings and formulating viable business models, established enterprises must be set up in a way that enables them to *think like a startup*. This means creating a company culture that embraces innovation, fosters agility in discovering new ways of creating market value and reacting to market changes, and motivates and empowers employees to identify market opportunities and develop offerings to address them.

Creating a Viable Business Model

Having a business model, while necessary, does not guarantee success. The business model must be viable: It must enable the company to create and capture value in the market in which it competes. To this end, a business model is guided by three imperatives: *focus*, *structure*, and *agility*.

Focus

An old Japanese proverb says: *Vision without action is a daydream. Action without vision is a nightmare.* This is particularly true in business. A company is unlikely to succeed unless it has a clear vision of the ultimate outcome it aims to achieve. Having a focus and a well-defined goal are prerequisites for developing a viable business model that ensures a company's success.

The business model is first and foremost focused on creating *market value*. Value is not limited to profits; it reflects the benefits and costs—monetary or nonmonetary—that a company creates and captures in a given market. The business model is not just a company's profit formula and is not only about making money. The business model is about creating *value*, be it monetary or not. Nonprofit enterprises have a business model even though their ultimate goal is not defined in financial terms.

The business model is not only about how the company creates value for its stakeholders. It is also about how the company creates value for its customers and collaborators. It is by creating value for its customers and collaborators that the company is able to create value for its stakeholders.

Structure

Although the ways in which companies create market value vary, the business models underlying their market success share a number of similarities. These similarities are captured by a common *framework* that serves as the backbone of the business model and is the foundation for the company's strategic and tactical decisions.

A framework facilitates business decisions in several ways. It delineates a general approach to identifying market opportunities. It enables managers to sidestep the trial-and-error-based learning process by outlining strategies for developing successful market offerings. It also facilitates teamwork by providing a shared vocabulary for the managers involved in the decision process.

A framework does not offer specific answers. Rather, it provides a general approach that helps identify opportunities and offer viable solutions to the problems faced by the company. Using a framework enables managers to evaluate the market opportunity, structure the business problem, parse their different components, and develop a sound solution. Following a framework is not a necessary condition for market success; there are companies that have succeeded merely by following the intuition of their top executives. Such companies, however, are an exception rather than the rule. A company that lacks a clearly articulated business model is more likely to fail than succeed.

Following a framework when developing a new business model might seem paradoxical. After all, generating a new business model calls for creativity and thinking outside the box. And a framework is, well, the box. This apparent contradiction raises the question: *Can one be truly creative when following a framework?* Absolutely. The purpose of a framework is not to constrain managers' creativity but to channel this creativity into a format that is most likely to lead to market success. Creativity in itself is not the ultimate focus of the business model; creating market value is. A value-focused framework can help turn creativity into a business success.

Agility

The conventional wisdom suggests that *no business model survives the first contact with the market.* There is much truth to this statement. The uncertainty associated with new product development and the constantly evolving nature of the market makes it challenging to develop a business model that will work out of the box. The uncertainty associated with many markets and their fluid nature raises the question: *Does the need for agility in a constantly changing world make business models unnecessary?*

The key to market success is not only generating a viable business model but also adapting this model to the changes in the market. Companies that fail to adapt their business models to a new market reality fade away, their businesses engulfed by companies with superior business models better equipped to create market value.

Agility does not imply absence of a business model; it means having a dynamic business model that adapts to changes in the environment. Agility involves seeking information to reduce market uncertainty and acting on this information by adapting a company's business model to the new market conditions. Agility is not a substitute for a business model; it is an integral component of the business model. Agility without a focus and structure amounts to chaos.

What does agility mean for a company's business model? The agile company thinks big, starts small, and scales fast. It is built on a series of small successes and failures rather than on a single big project that will likely collapse if the market conditions change. *The agile company takes risks, learns from failure, and pivots quickly by updating its business model in response to the market conditions.* The agile company understands that the only constant in business is change, and incorporates change into the design of its business model.

THE BUSINESS MODEL FRAMEWORK

*Each problem that I solved became a rule that
served afterwards to solve other problems.*
—René Descartes, French philosopher,
mathematician, and scientist

Each business model is unique: It outlines how a particular enterprise will address a specific customer need in a given market at a certain point in time. Despite their uniqueness, successful business models are built on the same core principles. These principles apply to both startups and established companies, to companies that are privately owned as well as those that are publicly traded, to high-tech and low-tech companies, to companies involved in manufacturing as well as to companies providing services.

The key aspects of a business model are captured in a framework that outlines the basic concepts common to successful market ventures, articulates the relationships among these concepts, and delineates the way in which business enterprises create market value. This framework, referred to as the *Market Value Framework*, defines the business model as comprising three building blocks: *target market, value proposition*, and *market offering*.

- The **target market** defines the market in which the company aims to create value. The target market is defined by five factors: *customers* whose needs the company aims to fulfill, *competitors* that aim to fulfill the same needs of the same target customers, *collaborators* that work with the company to fulfill target customers' needs, the *company* managing the offering, and the *context* in which the company operates.

- The **value proposition** defines the value that the company aims to create in the target market. The value proposition has three components—*customer value, collaborator value*, and *company value*—which reflect the value created by the company for the relevant market entities. Creating a meaningful *value proposition* is central to the development of a viable business model and is the key to market success.

- The **market offering** defines the actual good that the company deploys in the market to fulfill the needs of its target customers. The market offering is characterized by seven key attributes: *product, service, brand, price, incentives, communication*, and *distribution*.

The components of the business model are logically connected: The company develops an *offering* for a given *target market* to create *value* for its customers, collaborators, and the company. Because the key purpose of a business model is to outline the way in which a

[handwritten margin note: BACKBONE OF THE BUS. MODEL]

9

company's offering will create market value, the *value proposition* is the backbone of the business model.

The Market Value Framework

The three building blocks of the business model — the target market, value proposition, and market offering — define its *strategy* and the *tactics*.

- The strategy reflects a company's choice of the market in which it will compete and the value it intends to create in this market. Thus, the target market and the value proposition are the two key components of the strategic aspect of the business model.

- The tactics reflect the specific *offering* with which the company will create value in the chosen market. The tactics logically follow from the company's strategy and reflect the way the company will make this strategy a market reality. The tactics are defined by the seven attributes of the market offering: product, service, brand, price, incentives, communication, and distribution.

The three key components of the business model — the target market, value proposition, and market offering — and the processes involved in creating market value are discussed in detail in the following chapters.

THE TARGET MARKET

*There is only one boss. The customer. And he can fire
everybody in the company from the chairman on down,
simply by spending his money somewhere else.*

—Sam Walton, founder of Walmart

The target market is the market in which a company aims to create and capture value.
It is defined by five factors: *customers* whose needs the company aims to fulfill, *competitors* that aim to fulfill the same needs of the same target customers, *collaborators* that
work with the company to fulfill customers' needs, the *company* managing the offering,
and the *context* in which the company operates.

The five market factors are often referred to as the *Five Cs*, and the resulting framework
is referred to as the *5-C framework*. The 5-C framework can be visually represented by a
set of concentric ellipses, with target customers in the center; collaborators, competitors,
and the company in the middle; and the context on the outside. The central placement of
target customers reflects their defining role in the market; the other three entities—the
company, its collaborators, and its competitors—aim to create value for these customers.
The context is the outer layer because it defines the environment in which customers, the
company, its collaborators, and its competitors operate.

The Target Market (The 5-C Framework)

The five Cs and the relationships among them are discussed in more detail in the following sections.

Target Customers

Target customers are the entities (organizations or individuals) whose needs the company aims to fulfill. In business-to-consumer markets, target customers are the individuals who are typically the end users of the company's offerings. In business-to-business markets, target customers are other businesses that use the company's offerings. Target customers are defined by two factors: *needs* and *profile*.

- Customer needs reflect the specific problem (or problems) faced by customers that the company aims to address. Customer needs determine the benefits that customers expect to receive from the company's offering. Because customer needs are unobservable, identifying customers with a particular need can be a challenging task.

- Customer profile reflects customers' observable characteristics: *demographics* such as age, gender, income, occupation, education, religion, ethnicity, nationality, employment, social class, household size, and family life cycle; *geolocation* such as customers' permanent residence and their current location at a particular point in time; *psychographics* such as customers' personality, including moral values, attitudes, interests, and lifestyles; and *behavior* such as shopping habits, purchase frequency, purchase quantity, price sensitivity, sensitivity to promotional activities, loyalty, and social and leisure activities.

Both factors—needs and profile—are important in defining target customers. Customer needs determine the value the company must create for these customers, and the customer profile identifies effective and cost-efficient ways in which the company can reach customers with these needs to communicate and deliver its offering.

Consider the following examples of customers of two popular offerings: the iPhone and Starbucks.

iPhone fulfills customers' *need* for an all-in-one, always-on device that enables them to work, have fun, socialize, and even show off. Customers with this need tend to have diverse *profiles*: their ages range from teenagers to adults; they span social classes, income groups, and geographic locations; and they vary in occupation, hobbies, and lifestyles.

Starbucks fulfills customers' *need* for a place between home and work where they can enjoy indulgent coffee drinks crafted to their personal taste, relax, and socialize. Customers with these needs have different *profiles*: Most are adult urbanites aged 25 to 40 with a relatively high income, professional careers, and a sense of social responsibility; the second largest customer segment is young adults aged 16 to 24, many of whom are college students or young professionals.

The choice of target customers determines all other aspects of the market, including the scope of the competition, potential collaborators, company resources necessary to fulfill customer needs, and the context in which the company will create market value. A change in target customers typically leads to a change in competitors and collaborators, requires different company resources, and is influenced by different context factors. Because of its strategic importance in defining the market in which the company creates and captures value, choosing the right target customers is the key to building a successful business model. The processes of identifying target customers are discussed in more detail in the *Business Model Toolbox* section of this book.

Competitors

Competitors are entities that aim to fulfill the same need of the same customers as the company does. Competitors are defined relative to customer needs, not merely based on the industry within which they operate. For example, digital camera manufacturers not only compete with one another; they also compete with the manufacturers of smartphones because both digital cameras and smartphones can fulfill the same customer need of capturing a moment in time.

Companies compete with one another through the offerings they develop to fulfill the same need of the same customers. Because competition is customer-specific, companies that compete in one market can collaborate in another. For example, Apple competes with Microsoft in the market for personal computers and tablets while also collaborating with it to develop productivity software, including word processing and spreadsheet programs.

To illustrate, some of the key iPhone and Starbucks competitors are as follows:

iPhone competes with smartphones from other manufacturers, including Samsung, HTC, Sony, LG, and Google. It also competes with cameras from Canon, Fuji, Nikon, Sony, and Panasonic, as well as with portable music players from Sony, Pioneer, SanDisk, and Apple (iPod). It even competes with portable game consoles by enabling consumers to play games on their phones.

Starbucks competes with other chain stores offering drip- and espresso-based coffee drinks, including Dunkin' Donuts, McDonald's, Costa Coffee, and Peet's Coffee. It also competes with boutique coffee shops offering handcrafted coffee drinks. Starbucks also competes with offerings from the likes of Nespresso and Keurig, whose capsule-based technology enables consumers to easily make drip and espresso coffee drinks at home. Finally, Starbucks competes with traditional coffee producers including Folgers, Maxwell House, and Eight O'Clock Coffee.

Collaborators

Collaborators are entities that work with the company to create value for target customers. The choice of collaborators is driven by the complementarity of the resources needed to fulfill customer needs. Collaboration involves outsourcing (rather than developing) the resources that the company lacks and that are needed to fulfill the needs of its target customers. Thus, instead of building or acquiring resources that are lacking, a company can "borrow" them by partnering with entities that have these resources and can benefit from sharing them.

Common types of collaborators include suppliers, manufacturers, distributors (dealers, wholesalers, and retailers), research-and-development entities, service providers, external sales force, advertising agencies, and marketing research companies. For example, Procter & Gamble collaborates with the design firm IDEO to develop some of its products, with Diamond Packaging to provide packaging, and with retail giant Walmart for distribution. Walmart collaborates with Procter & Gamble to procure many of its products, with software solutions provider Oracle to streamline its logistics, and with shipping conglomerate Moller-Maersk to transport its goods.

Consider the collaborator networks of Apple and Starbucks:

iPhone benefits from Apple's collaboration with wireless service providers such as AT&T, Verizon, T-Mobile, and Sprint that ensure compatibility of the iPhone across different wireless networks. Apple also collaborates with numerous suppliers such as 3M, Corning, Intel, Foxconn, LG, Samsung, and Qualcomm. In addition, Apple collaborates with various retailers such as Walmart, Target, and Best Buy that make the iPhone available to the public.

Starbucks collaborates with numerous coffee growers around the globe to provide high-quality coffee beans. Starbucks also partners with suppliers that provide various non-coffee items such as water, pastries, snacks, and branded merchandise. In addition, Starbucks collaborates with a variety of retail outlets including grocery chains, mass-merchandisers, warehouse clubs, and convenience stores that sell Starbucks coffee beans, instant coffee, and snacks.

Company

The company is the entity that develops and manages a given market offering. The company can be a manufacturer that produces the actual goods being sold (Procter & Gamble), a service provider (American Express), an entity engaged in brand building (Lacoste), a media company (Facebook), or a retailer (Walmart). The company is not limited to a single activity; it can perform multiple functions. For example, a retailer might have its own production facility, engage in building its own brand, and offer a variety of value-added services.

In the case of enterprises with diverse strategic competencies and market offerings, the term *company* refers to the particular business unit (often referred to as the *strategic business unit*) of the organization managing the specific offering. For example, General Electric, Alphabet (formerly Google), and Facebook have multiple strategic business units, each of which can be viewed as a separate company requiring its own business model.

The company is defined by two key factors: *profile* and *goals*:

- **Profile** reflects the company's characteristics, including the resources that determine its ability to create market value and a sustainable competitive advantage. A company's resources include factors such as business facilities; suppliers; employees; know-how; existing products, services, and brands; communication and distribution channels; and access to capital.

- **Goals** reflect the end result that the company aims to achieve with a particular offering. Company goals can be monetary, such as maximizing profits, and/or strategic, such as creating synergies with other company offerings and creating value for society at large.

To illustrate, the profile and goals of Apple and Starbucks are as follows:

iPhone's (Apple's) *profile* is characterized by its production facilities; its relationships with suppliers, manufacturers, and distributors; its technology-savvy employees, its intellectual property including know-how, patents, and trademarks; its strong brand; its existing product and service ecosystem; its loyal customer base; and its vast cash reserves. The iPhone's *goals* are to be Apple's key revenue and profit driver (monetary goal) and a cornerstone of Apple's ecosystem of products and services (strategic goal).

Starbucks' *profile* is defined by its numerous retail locations, its relationships with coffee growers and distributors, its professionally trained employees, its intellectual property, its strong brand, its loyal customer base, and access to capital markets. Starbucks' *monetary goal* — to generate revenues and profits for its shareholders — is complemented by its *strategic goal* to benefit society and promote social responsibility.

Context

Context describes the environment in which the company operates. It is defined by five factors:

- **Sociocultural context** includes social and demographic trends, value systems, religion, language, lifestyles, attitudes, and beliefs.
- **Technological context** includes new techniques, skills, methods, and processes for designing, manufacturing, communicating, and delivering market offerings.
- **Regulatory context** includes taxes; import tariffs; embargoes; product specification, pricing, and communication regulations; and intellectual property laws.
- **Economic context** includes economic growth, money supply, inflation, and interest rates.
- **Physical context** includes natural resources, climate, geographic location, topography, and health trends.

To illustrate, consider the context in which iPhone and Starbucks operate:

iPhone's context is characterized by people's mounting desire for mobile connectivity that enables them to search, share, and shop on the go; by rapid technological developments including the availability and speed of wireless connectivity, improved battery life and processing speed, and enhanced image processing; by intellectual property laws enabling the company to protect its patents, trade secrets, and trademarks; and by the overall economic conditions that determine customers' disposable income.

Starbucks' context is characterized by the growing popularity of crafted coffee drinks and the desire to socialize in person, as well as by the growing popularity of online communications; by the technological developments that enable the company to better understand its customers, track their buying behavior, and communicate with them on a one-on-one basis; by the favorable trade agreements that influence import tariffs on coffee; by various economic factors including the state of the local economy and the global commodity prices for coffee; as well as by the climate and weather patterns across different geographic locations.

THE VALUE PROPOSITION

Good companies meet needs; great companies create markets.
— Philip Kotler, founder of modern marketing theory

To succeed, an offering must create superior value for all relevant entities involved in the market exchange—target customers, collaborators, and the company. Accordingly, when developing market offerings, a company needs to consider all three types of value: *customer value*, *collaborator value*, and *company value*. These three types of value are discussed in detail below.

The Customer Value Proposition

Customer value is the worth of an offering to its customers; it is customers' assessment of the degree to which an offering fulfills their needs. The value an offering creates for its customers is determined by three main factors: (1) the *needs* of these customers, (2) the intrinsic value created by the company's offering, and (3) the value created by the alternative means (competitive offerings) these customers can use to fulfill their needs. Simply put, the customer value proposition answers the question: *Why would target customers choose the company's offering instead of the available alternatives?*

The Customer Value Proposition

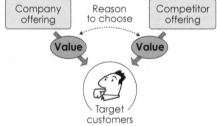

The customer value proposition of an offering can be described in terms of its similarity to and differences from the competitive offerings. Specifically, the value proposition can be defined on three dimensions: *points of dominance*, *points of parity*, and *points of compromise*.

- **Points of dominance** (PoD) are the dimensions on which a company's offering is superior to the competition. For example, an offering might have higher reliability, greater comfort, and better performance than the competition.

- **Points of parity** (PoP) are the dimensions on which a company's offering is equal to the competition. For example, an offering's durability might be identical to that of its competitors.

- **Points of compromise** (PoC) are the dimensions on which a company's offering is inferior to the competition. These are the attributes on which customers must compromise in order to receive the unique benefits afforded by the offering. For example, customers might compromise on price in order to gain higher levels of reliability, comfort, and performance.

Each of the above dimensions—points of dominance, points of parity, and points of compromise—reflect the way customers *perceive* the market offerings rather than their actual performance. For example, a product associated with a strong brand might be perceived to have superior performance compared to a functionally identical generic product, thus creating a point of dominance. Because value is in the eyes of the beholder, the value proposition is determined by the way customers perceive the offering and not necessarily by its actual performance.

An offering can create customer value on three dimensions: *functional, psychological,* and *monetary.*

- **Functional value** reflects the benefits and costs directly related to an offering's practical utility such as performance, reliability, durability, compatibility, ease of use, design, and customization. The functional value of an offering is given by the answer to the question: *How does the offering's functionality benefit target customers?*

- **Psychological value** reflects the mental benefits and costs of the offering, such as the emotional experience provided by the offering and the offering's ability to signal a customer's social status and personality. The psychological value of an offering is given by the answer to the question: *How do target customers feel about the offering?*

- **Monetary value** reflects the financial benefits and costs of the offering, such as its price, fees, discounts, and rebates, as well as the various monetary costs associated with using, maintaining, and disposing of the offering. The monetary value of an offering is given by the answer to the question: *What is the monetary impact of the offering on target customers?*

Dimensions of Customer Value

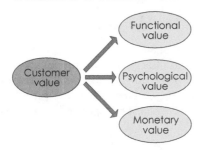

The three dimensions of customer value are illustrated by the following examples:

iPhone. The *functional value* of the iPhone is defined by its mobile connectivity; its ability to make phone calls, send text messages, and take pictures; and the benefits offered by millions of productivity and entertainment apps. Its *psychological value* stems from the satisfaction of using an aesthetically pleasing, user-friendly device; from peace of mind that the iPhone will function as described; and from the iPhone's ability to convey one's personality and social status. Finally, the iPhone's *monetary value* is defined by its price and any available promotional incentives.

Starbucks. The *functional value* of Starbucks is defined by its ability to provide energy (caffeine) and promote productivity, as well as offer a physical space in which to relax, work, and socialize. The *psychological value* stems from the sensual pleasure of consuming Starbucks beverages and snacks, the ability of customers to express their identity through their choice of a handcrafted beverage created just for them, as well as the feeling of moral satisfaction derived from supporting a socially responsible company. Finally, Starbucks' *monetary value* is reflected in its prices and various monetary incentives, including loyalty points, buy-one-get-one offers, and promotional discounts.

Tesla. The *functional value* of Tesla electric cars includes speed, safety, acceleration, and comfort. The *psychological value* stems from the satisfaction of preserving the environment, the exhilaration of experiencing the car's acceleration, and the sense of self-fulfillment associated with owning a prestigious car. Finally, the *monetary value* is determined by the car's price, maintenance costs, and fuel savings.

Gillette. The *functional value* of Gillette razors is defined by the clean, smooth, and comfortable shave they offer to customers. The *psychological value* stems from the satisfaction of using a technologically advanced shaving system promoted as "The Best a Man Can Get." Finally, the *monetary value* is determined by the price of Gillette's razors and cartridges.

The dimensions of customer value are not universally positive. Because value stems from both benefits and costs, on a particular dimension costs might outweigh the benefits. In most cases, the functional value and psychological value, which reflect the core benefits of the offering, are positive, whereas the monetary value, which involves the price paid by consumers for the offering, is negative. To create customer value, the benefits across all three dimensions should outweigh the corresponding costs.

The Collaborator Value Proposition

Collaborator value is the worth of an offering to the company's collaborators; it is the sum of all benefits and costs that an offering creates for collaborators. The collaborator value proposition reflects an offering's ability to fulfill collaborator goals better than the alternative offerings. Simply put, the collaborator value proposition answers the question: *Why would collaborators choose the company's offering instead of the competitive alternatives?*

The Collaborator Value Proposition

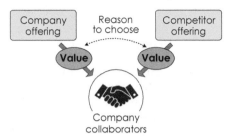

As in the case of the customer value proposition, the collaborator value proposition can be defined on three dimensions: *points of dominance* (dimensions on which the company's offering provides its collaborators with benefits that are superior to those of the competitive offering), *points of parity* (dimensions on which the collaborator benefits of the company's offering are equal to those of the competition), and *points of compromise* (dimensions on which the company's offering provides collaborators with benefits that are inferior to those of the competition).

A company's offering can create two types of collaborator value: *monetary* and *strategic*.

- **Monetary value** involves the monetary benefits and costs—such as net income, profit margins, sales revenue, earnings per share, and return on investment—that an offering creates for the company's collaborators.

- **Strategic value** involves nonmonetary benefits and costs that are of strategic importance to company collaborators. An offering can create strategic value by promoting collaborators' other offerings, by strengthening collaborators' brands, and by providing collaborators with relevant market information. For example, a retailer can benefit from carrying a manufacturer's product that is in high demand because it generates store traffic. Likewise, an offering can create strategic value by enabling the company's collaborators to leverage the offering's brand to strengthen their own offerings.

Dimensions of Collaborator Value

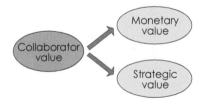

The collaborator value proposition can be illustrated with the following examples:

iPhone. Wireless service providers receive the strategic benefit of associating their service with a product that is in high demand and is likely to promote greater usage of wireless services. Retailers receive monetary benefit from selling the iPhone as well as the strategic benefit of carrying a traffic-generating product.

Starbucks. Coffee growers receive monetary payments for the coffee beans and the strategic benefit of having a consistent demand for their offerings. Retailers receive monetary benefit from selling Starbucks products as well as the strategic benefit of carrying a traffic-generating product.

The Company Value Proposition

Company value is the worth of the offering to the company; it is the sum of all benefits and costs associated with an offering. As is the case with customer and collaborator value, the value of an offering is often defined relative to the other opportunities that are available to the company. For example, when assessing the viability of a new offering, its value is typically benchmarked against the value of other offerings that could be launched by the company. Here, the reference point against which its value to the company is assessed is the opportunity cost of developing a given offering instead of an alternative offering. The company value proposition answers the question: *Why would the company choose this offering instead of the alternative options?*

The Company Value Proposition

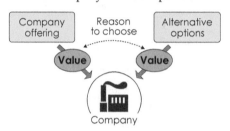

As with the customer and collaborator value propositions, an offering's value proposition for the company can be described in terms of *points of dominance* (dimensions on which an offering is superior to the alternative options), *points of parity* (dimensions on which an offering is equivalent to the alternative options), and *points of compromise* (dimensions on which an offering is inferior to the alternative options).

Furthermore, as in the case of collaborator value, an offering can create two types of value for the company: *monetary* and *strategic*.

- **Monetary value** reflects the monetary benefits and costs of the offering and is typically expressed in financial terms such as net income, profit margins, sales revenue, earnings per share, and return on investment. Monetary value is the most common type of value sought by for-profit companies. The ways in which an offering creates monetary value for the company is referred to as the *profit formula* and is discussed in more detail in the *Business Model Toolbox* section of this book.

- **Strategic value** involves nonmonetary benefits and costs that are of strategic importance to the company. An offering can create strategic value by facilitating the demand for other offerings in the company's portfolio, by strengthening the company's reputation, and by providing the company with information about its target customers. For example, a free software app can create value for the company by providing it with a technological platform for developing high-margin offerings, promoting the company's brand, and gaining information about customers' preferences, demographics, and behavior.

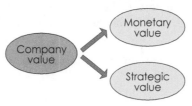

The different dimensions of company value can be illustrated with the following examples:

iPhone. Apple receives monetary compensation (revenues and profits) from selling the iPhone. The iPhone also delivers the strategic benefit of creating a strong consumer brand, strengthening Apple's other brands, and expanding its ecosystem of compatible products and services.

Starbucks derives monetary benefit (revenues and profits) from selling its products and services to its customers. Starbucks also receives the strategic benefit of creating a strong consumer brand, enhancing its market footprint, and broadening its portfolio of offerings.

The Market Value Principle

To succeed, a company must create value for three market entities: target customers, the company, and its collaborators. To this end, the company's value proposition must follow the *market value principle*:

> *The company must create superior value for its target customers*
> *and collaborators in a way that enables it to achieve its goals*

The market value principle means that the viability of a business model is defined by the answers to three sets of questions:

What value does the offering create for its target customers? Why would target customers choose this offering? What makes this offering better than the alternative options?

What value does the offering create for the company's collaborators? Why would the entities identified as collaborators (suppliers, distributors, and co-developers) partner with the company?

What value does the offering create for the company? Why should the company invest resources in this offering rather than in an alternative offering?

The Market Value Principle

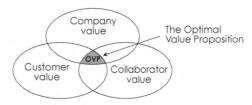

The ability to create superior value for customers, collaborators, and the company is the ultimate criterion for market success. Failure to create superior value for any of these entities inevitably leads to an unsustainable business model and a failure of the business venture.

The market value principle and the concept of the optimal value proposition can be illustrated with the following examples:

iPhone. *Customers* receive the functionality and prestige of the iPhone, for which they offer Apple and its collaborators monetary compensation. *Collaborators* (wireless service providers) receive the strategic benefit of associating their service with a product that is in high demand and likely to promote greater usage of wireless services. In return, these collaborators invest resources in making their services compatible with the iPhone. Another set of collaborators (retailers) receives monetary benefit (profits) from selling the iPhone as well as the strategic benefit of carrying a traffic-generating product. Retailers then invest monetary and strategic resources (shelf space, inventory management, and sales force) to ensure that the iPhone is available to its customers. In return for developing, advertising, and distributing the iPhone, the *company* (Apple) receives monetary compensation from consumers purchasing the iPhone as well as the strategic benefit of strengthening its consumer brand and its ecosystem of compatible Apple products.

Starbucks. *Customers* receive the functional benefit of a variety of coffee beverages as well as the psychological benefit of expressing certain aspects of their personality through the choice of a customized beverage, for which they deliver monetary compensation. Starbucks *collaborators* (coffee growers) receive monetary payments for the coffee beans they provide and the strategic benefit of having a consistent demand for their product, in return for which they invest resources in growing coffee beans that conform to Starbucks' standards. By investing resources in developing and offering its products and services to consumers, the company (Starbucks) derives monetary benefit (revenues and profits) and the strategic benefit of building a consumer brand and enhancing its market footprint and portfolio of offerings.

Uber. *Customers* (riders) receive the core benefit (transportation), convenience (short wait time), and comfort (better service), for which they offer monetary compensation. *Collaborators* (drivers) receive monetary compensation and flexible working hours, for which they transport customers to their destination. The *company* (Uber) receives a share of customer revenues and in return provides the informational, logistical, promotional, and legal infrastructure connecting drivers and riders.

Google. *Customers* receive information, for which they pay by sharing information about their needs, preferences, and behaviors and by viewing the advertisements embedded in the information they receive. *Collaborators* (advertisers) have the ability to promote their offerings, generate traffic, and gather customer information, for which they pay Google. In return for building and managing its search engine and data analytics, *Google* receives information from customers about their needs, preferences, and behaviors as well as monetary compensation from its collaborators.

THE MARKET OFFERING

Strategy without tactics is the slowest route to victory.
Tactics without strategy is the noise before defeat.

—Sun Tzu, Chinese military strategist

The market offering is the actual good that the company deploys to fulfill a particular customer need. Unlike the target market and the value proposition, which define the strategy underlying the company's business model, the market offering reflects its tactics — the specific way in which the company creates market value.

The Seven Attributes Defining the Market Offering

A company's offering is defined by seven attributes: product, service, brand, price, incentives, communication, and distribution. These seven attributes are the business model tactics — the specific activities employed to execute the offering's strategy. The tactics are the means that managers have at their disposal to create market value.

An offering's strategy and tactics, although logically connected, are two distinct aspects of the business model. The strategy defines the target market and the value the company aims to create in this market. The tactics, on the other hand, define the attributes of the offering that is being exchanged in the market. Unlike strategy, which is unobservable to the public, the tactics can be readily observed by the company's customers and competitors.

Creating Market Value: Strategy and Tactics

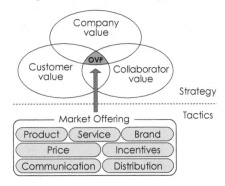

The seven attributes defining the market offering can be described as follows:

- The **product** aspect of an offering reflects the benefits of the good with which the company aims to create market value. Products can be both tangible (e.g., food, apparel, and automobiles) and intangible (e.g., software, music, and video). Products typically entitle customers to permanent rights to the acquired good. For example, a customer purchasing a car or a software program takes ownership of the acquired product.

- The **service** aspect of an offering reflects the benefits of the good with which the company aims to create value for its customers without entitling them to permanent ownership of this good (e.g., movie rental, appliance repairs, medical procedures, and tax preparation). The service aspect of the offering is closely related to its product aspect such that some offerings might be positioned as either a product or a service. For example, a software can be offered as a product, with customers purchasing the rights to a copy of the program, or as a service, with customers renting the program to temporarily receive its benefits. Many offerings involve both product and service components. For example, a mobile phone offering includes a product component—the physical device that customers acquire—as well as a service component that includes wireless connectivity and device repairs.

- The **brand** is a marketing tool that aims to inform customers about the source of the products and services associated with the brand. The brand helps identify the company's products and services, differentiate them from those of the competition, and create unique value beyond the product and service aspects of the offering. For example, the Harley-Davidson brand identifies its motorcycles; differentiates these motorcycles from those made by Honda, Suzuki, Kawasaki, and Yamaha; and elicits a distinct emotional reaction from its customers, who use Harley-Davidson's brand to express their individuality.

- The **price** is the amount of money the company charges its customers and collaborators for the benefits provided by the offering.

- **Incentives** are tools that enhance the value of the offering by reducing its costs and/or by increasing its benefits. Common incentives include volume discounts, price reductions, coupons, rebates, premiums, bonus offerings, contests, and rewards. Incentives can be offered to individual customers, the company's collaborators (e.g., incentives given to channel partners), and the company's employees.

- **Communication** informs the relevant market entities—target customers, collaborators, and the company's employees and stakeholders—about the specifics of the offering.

- **Distribution** defines the channel(s) used to deliver the offering to target customers and the company's collaborators.

The seven attributes defining the market offering are the tools managers use to create value; they are the actionable aspects of the company's business model. The offering attributes can be thought of as the levers that managers use to execute the desired strategy to achieve the company's ultimate goal.

The key attributes defining the offering are illustrated by the following examples:

iPhone. The *product* is the actual phone, defined by its physical characteristics and functionality. The *service* is the wireless connectivity provided by the phone companies as well as the assistance offered by Apple in using and repairing the phone. The *brand* is the iPhone identity—its name, logo, and the associations that it evokes in people's minds. The *price* is the amount of money Apple charges for the iPhone. *Incentives* are the promotional tools such as temporary price reductions that provide additional value for iPhone customers. *Communication* is the information conveyed by press conferences, media coverage, and advertisements that inform the public about the iPhone. *Distribution* encompasses the channels—Apple's own stores and authorized resellers—that make the iPhone available to the public.

Starbucks. The *product* is the variety of coffee and other beverages, as well as food items available. The *service* is the assistance offered to customers prior to, during, and after purchase. The *brand* is Starbucks' name, logo, and the associations it evokes in customers' minds. The *price* is the monetary amount that Starbucks charges customers for its offerings. *Incentives* are the promotional tools—loyalty program, coupons, and temporary price reductions—that provide additional benefits for customers. *Communication* is the information disseminated via different media channels—advertising, social media, and public relations—informing the public about Starbucks. *Distribution* involves the channels through which Starbucks' offerings are delivered to its customers: Starbucks-owned stores and retail outlets licensed to carry Starbucks' products.

The Offering as a Means of Creating Customer Value

The seven attributes defining the market offering—product, service, brand, price, incentives, communication, and distribution—can be viewed as a *process of designing, communicating, and delivering* customer value. The product, service, brand, price, and incentives are the value-design aspect of the offering; communication is the process of communicating value, and distribution is the value-delivery aspect of the offering. Customer value is created across all three dimensions, with different attributes playing distinct roles in the value-creation process.

The Market Offering as a Process of Designing, Communicating, and Delivering Customer Value

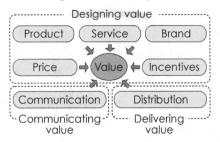

Because they define the key benefits and costs of the offering, the product, service, brand, price, and incentives are the key value drivers of the offering. Communication and distribution are the channels through which the benefits created by the first five attributes are communicated and delivered to target customers. Thus, communication informs customers of the functionality of a product or service, builds the image of its brand, publicizes its price, apprises buyers of sales promotions, and advises them about the availability of the offering. Likewise, distribution delivers a company's products and services, delivers customer payments to the company, and delivers the offering's promotional incentives to customers and collaborators.

The value-creation process can be examined from both the company and customer perspectives. From a company's perspective, value creation is a process of *designing, communicating,* and *delivering* value. From a customer's perspective, however, the value-creation process can be viewed in terms of the *attractiveness, awareness,* and *availability* of the offering. Thus, an offering's ability to create customer value is given by the answers to the following three questions:

What makes the offering attractive to target customers?

How will target customers become aware of the offering?

How will target customers acquire the offering?

The answer to the first question outlines the customer benefits and costs associated with the product, service, brand, price, and incentives aspects of the offering. The answer to the second question outlines the way in which the company will communicate the product, service, brand, price, and incentives aspects of the offering to its target customers to make them aware of the offering. The answer to the third question outlines the way in which the company will make the offering available to its target customers. Thus, the customer-centric approach to managing the *attractiveness, awareness,* and *availability* of an offering complements the company-centric approach of managing the processes of *designing, communicating,* and *delivering* value to target customers.

Company Actions and Customer Impact

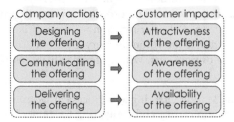

To illustrate the process of designing, communicating, and delivering value, consider the following examples:

iPhone. The *product* aspect of managing Apple's offering involves designing the iPhone, communicating its benefits to consumers, and then physically delivering it to buyers. The *service* aspect of the iPhone involves designing the key aspects of the services (Apple's own service and that of the wireless carriers) it offers to customers, communicating these services to target customers, and ultimately delivering these services to buyers. Building the iPhone *brand* involves creating the iPhone name, designing the logo, and defining the image that Apple wants to be associated with the iPhone in people's minds—and then communicating and delivering this brand to consumers. Furthermore, Apple has to set the iPhone *price*, communicate this price to potential buyers, and then "deliver" the price by collecting payments from consumers. Finally, with respect to *incentives*, Apple has to decide on the type of sales promotions to use, communicate these promotions to potential buyers, and then deliver these promotions to target customers.

Starbucks. The *product* aspect of Starbucks' offerings involves designing its portfolio of products—espressos, lattes, macchiatos, and frappuccinos—informing and educating customers about these drinks, and then physically delivering them to customers. The *service* aspect of the offering involves defining the level of service that Starbucks wants to offer customers, communicating its service policies (such as the promise that a customer's drink will be perfect every time), and ultimately delivering the service to its customers. Building the Starbucks *brand* involves selecting the brand name, designing its logo, defining what Starbucks wants it to mean to its customers (Starbucks' goal is to become the "third place" in people's daily lives, after home and work), and then communicating and delivering this meaning to target customers. With respect to *price*, Starbucks has to set prices for all possible combinations of its various drinks and sizes, communicate these prices to consumers (e.g., by displaying them in its stores), collect consumer payments, and transfer them to the company's bank. Finally, Starbucks has to decide what, when, and how many *incentives* to offer (such as discounts on certain drinks, 2-for-1 promotions, and loyalty programs), create awareness of these incentives by communicating them to customers, and then deliver them to target customers using appropriate channels (e.g., newspaper inserts, online banner advertisements, and proximity-based mobile promotions).

The key principle in developing the market offering is to ensure that the different attributes of the offering—product, service, brand, price, incentives, communication, and distribution—are aligned with the offering's strategy. To this end, a company must design, communicate, and deliver its offering in a way that creates superior value for target customers while benefiting the company and its collaborators.

THE MARKET VALUE MAP

Innovation is not the product of logical thought,
although the result is tied to logical structure.
— Albert Einstein, theoretical physicist

For practical purposes, a company's business model can be represented as a value map that outlines the specific ways in which an offering creates value for its target customers, collaborators, and the company. The primary purpose of a value map is to visually outline the key aspects of the business model and serve as a workbook that lays out the company's strategy and tactics. The key aspects of developing a market value map are outlined below, and detailed examples are given in the *Business Model Examples* section at the end of this book.

The Market Value Map

The market value map is a practical tool that delineates the ways in which an offering creates value for the relevant market entities—target customers, the company, and its collaborators. The market value map presents the business model in a schematic way, enabling managers to clearly articulate the key aspects of the company's business model. To this end, the market value map identifies the answers to the questions a manager should ask when designing new business models and when evaluating existing ones.

The market value map framework comprises the three core concepts—*the target market*, *the value proposition*, and *the market offering*—that define the offering's strategy and tactics. Accordingly, the market value map takes the shape of a matrix: The left side outlines the key elements of the business model strategy—the target market (customers, collaborators, company, competitors, and context) and the value proposition (customer value, collaborator value, and company value)—and the right side outlines the market offering defined by its seven key attributes (product, service, brand, price, incentives, communication, and distribution).

The key aspect of the market value map is the offering's value proposition, which delineates the value that the offering will create for target customers, collaborators, and the company. The development of the value proposition is guided by the market value principle: The offering must create superior value for target customers in a way that benefits the company and its collaborators.

The components of the market value map and the key questions defining each component are shown in the figure below and discussed in more detail in the next sections.

The Market Value Map

Target Market

Customers
What customer need does the company aim to fulfill? Who are the customers with this need?

Collaborators
What other entities will work with the company to fulfill the identified customer need?

Company
What are the company's resources that will enable it to fulfill the identified customer need?

Competition
What other offerings aim to fulfill the same need of the same target customers?

Context
What are the sociocultural, technological, regulatory, economic, and physical aspects of the environment?

Value Proposition

Customer Value
What value does the offering create for target customers?

Collaborator Value
What value does the offering create for the company's collaborators?

Company Value
What value does the offering create for the company?

Market Offering

Product
What are the key features of the company's product?

Service
What are the key features of the company's service?

Brand
What are the key features of the offering's brand?

Price
What is the offering's price?

Incentives
What incentives does the offering provide?

Communication
How will target customers and collaborators become aware of the company's offering?

Distribution
How will the offering be delivered to target customers and collaborators?

Strategy ← (Target Market / Value Proposition)

Tactics ← (Market Offering)

Target Market

The target market is the market in which a company aims to create and capture value. The target market comprises five key components: *customers, collaborators, company, competitors*, and *context*. To define the target market, a manager should ask five sets of questions:

What customer need does the company aim to fulfill? Who are the customers with this need?

What other entities will work with the company to fulfill the identified customer need?

What is the entity managing the offering? What are this entity's resources that will enable it to fulfill the identified customer need?

What other offerings aim to fulfill the same need of the same target customers?

What are the relevant sociocultural, technological, regulatory, economic, and physical aspects of the environment in which the company operates?

Value Proposition

The value proposition articulates the benefits and costs associated with the company's offering for the three relevant market entities: *target customers, collaborators,* and *the company.* The key questions here are:

What value does the offering create for target customers?

What value does the offering create for the company's collaborators?

What value does the offering create for the company?

Market Offering

The market offering is the actual good that the company introduces in a given market to create value for its target customers, collaborators, and company stakeholders. The market offering is defined by seven attributes: *product, service, brand, price, incentives, communication,* and *distribution.* To define the market offering, a manager should ask the following questions:

What are the key features of the product, service, brand, price, and incentives the company offers to its customers?

How will target customers become aware of the offering?

How will the offering be delivered to target customers? How will different attributes of the offering create customer value?

Customer, Collaborator, and Company Value Maps

The market value map offers an overview of the ways in which an offering creates value for the three relevant market entities — customers, collaborators, and the company. Because each of these entities requires its own value proposition and employs different tools to create value, the market value map can be represented as three separate maps: the customer value map, the collaborator value map, and the company value map.

These three value maps depict a company's business model from the viewpoint of each of the three market entities involved in the value-creation process. The *customer value map* reflects the way an offering creates value for target customers, the *collaborator value map* reflects the way an offering creates value for the company's collaborators, and the *company value map* reflects the way an offering creates value for the company.

The Customer Value Map

The customer value map outlines the way in which a company's offering can fulfill the needs of its target customers better than the competition can. The customer value map aims to address the question:

How does the company create superior value for its target customers?

The customer value map consists of four building blocks: *target customers, the competition, the customer value proposition,* and *the customer offering.* The core components of the customer value map are shown in the figure below and are outlined in more detail in the following sections.

The Customer Value Map

Target Customers		Customer Offering	
Customer need What customer need does the company aim to fulfill?		**Product** What are the features of the product that the company offers to target customers?	
Customer profile Who are the customers with this need?		**Service** What are the features of the service that the company offers to target customers?	
Competition		**Brand** What are the features of the offering's brand?	
Key competitors What other offerings aim to fulfill the same customer need?		**Price** What is the offering's price for target customers?	
Value proposition What value do these offerings create for target customers?		**Incentives** What incentives does the offering provide to target customers?	
Offering attributes What are the key aspects of the competitive offerings?		**Communication** How will target customers become aware of the company's offering?	
Customer Value		**Distribution** How will the offering be delivered to target customers?	
Reason to choose What value does the offering create for target customers? Why would they choose this offering?			

Target Customers

Target customers are the buyers for whom the company is developing its offering. Identifying target customers involves identifying an unmet *customer need* that the company intends to fulfill and defining the demographic and behavioral *profiles* of customers with this need. These two aspects are outlined below and discussed in more detail in the *Business Model Toolbox* section of this book.

- The **customer need** identifies a problem faced by customers that the company aims to address with its offering. The key questions here are: *What customer need does the offering aim to fulfill? How common is this need? Do customers view this need as a problem that has to be solved and actively seek alternative means to fulfill this need?*

- The **customer profile** identifies the observable characteristics of the target customers that the company could use to communicate and deliver the offering to these customers. The key questions here are: *Who are the customers that have the need the company aims to fulfill? What demographic characteristics and behaviors of these customers can the company use to reach them?*

Competition

The competition consists of the alternative offerings that fulfill the same need of the same customers as the company's offering. The competition is defined by the *key competitors*, their *value proposition* for target customers, and the *attributes of the competitive offerings*.

- **Key competitors** are the alternative means that target customers can use to achieve their goals. The key questions here are: *What means are target customers currently using to fulfill the identified need? If the company does not introduce its offering, what would these customers do? What product, service, or behavior does the company's offering aim to replace? What would target customers <u>not</u> choose if they were to choose the company's offering?*

- The **competitive value proposition** outlines the benefits and costs that competitive offerings create for target customers and the reasons why customers might prefer competitive offerings to those created by the company. The key questions here are: *What benefits do the competitive offerings create for target customers? What customer costs are associated with the competitive offerings?*

- The **attributes of the competitive offerings** involve their product, service, brand, price, incentives, communication, and distribution components. The key questions here are: *What are the product, service, brand, price, incentives, communication, and distribution aspects of the competitive offering? How do the attributes of the competitive offering create customer value?*

The Customer Value Proposition

The customer value proposition defines the worth of an offering to target customers. It is identified by the *customer value equation*, the *competitive advantage* of the company's offering, and the *reason* why customers would choose the company's offering.

- The **customer value equation** identifies the benefits and costs created by the offering on each of the three dimensions of customer value: functional, psychological, and monetary. The key question here is: *What functional, psychological, and monetary benefits and costs does the offering create for its target customers?*

- The **competitive advantage** is the ability of an offering to fulfill a particular customer need better than the alternative options. The key questions here are: *Why should target customers choose the company's offering instead of using alternative means of fulfilling the identified need? What are the points of dominance, points of parity, and points of compromise of the company's offering relative to the competitive offerings?*

- The **reason to choose** is a key factor(s) that will motivate customers to buy and use the company's offering. The key questions here are: *What is the primary reason for customers to choose the company offering? How would customers justify choosing the company's offering?*

Customer Offering

The customer offering is defined by the seven attributes—product, service, brand, price, incentives, communication, and distribution—that delineate the company's offering and the value that these attributes create for target customers. The key questions here are: *What are the key features of the product, service, brand, price, and incentives the company offers to its customers? How will target customers become aware of the offering? How will the offering be delivered to target customers? How will different attributes of the offering create customer value?*

The Collaborator Value Map

The collaborator value map outlines the ways in which an offering can help the company's collaborators achieve their goals better than the competitive offerings can. The collaborator value map aims to address the question:

How does the company create superior value for its collaborators?

Similar to the customer value map, the collaborator value map consists of four building blocks: *collaborators, the competition, the collaborator value proposition,* and *the collaborator offering*. The core components of the collaborator value map are shown in the figure below and are outlined in more detail in the following sections.

The Collaborator Value Map

Collaborators	Collaborator Offering
Collaborator profile — Which entities would partner with the company to create value for target customers?	**Product** — What are the features of the product that the company offers to collaborators?
Collaborator goals — What goals do collaborators pursue by partnering with the company?	**Service** — What are the features of the service that the company offers to collaborators?
Competition	**Brand** — What are the features of the offering's brand?
Key competitors — What other offerings aim to fulfill the same collaborator goals?	**Price** — What is the offering's price for collaborators?
Value proposition — What value do these offerings create for collaborators?	**Incentives** — What incentives does the offering provide to collaborators?
Offering attributes — What are the key aspects of the competitive offerings?	**Communication** — How will collaborators become aware of the company's offering?
Collaborator Value	
Reason to choose — What value does the offering create for collaborators? Why would they partner with the company?	**Distribution** — How will the offering be delivered to collaborators?

Key Collaborators

Collaborators are entities working with the company to create value for target customers. Identifying collaborators has two aspects: defining the *profile* of the partnering entities and their resources, and identifying the *goals* that these entities aim to achieve by partnering with the company.

- The **collaborator profile** reflects the key aspects of the partnering entity, such as resources, location, size, and industry. The key questions here are: *What resources needed to create superior value for target customers is the company looking to outsource? Which entities have the resources the company lacks and is looking to outsource? What are the key characteristics of these entities?*

- **Collaborator goals** are the outcomes that collaborators aim to achieve through collaboration. The key question here is: *What monetary and strategic goals do collaborators aim to achieve by partnering with the company?*

Competition

The competition consists of the alternative offerings that target the same goals of the same collaborators that the company does. The competition is defined by the *key competitors*, their *value proposition* for the collaborators, and the *attributes of the competitive offerings*.

- **Key competitors** are the alternative means that the company collaborators can use to achieve their goals. The key questions here are: *What are potential collaborators currently doing to achieve their goals? If they do not partner with the company, what will these collaborators do? What offering does the company aim to replace with its offering?*

- The **competitive value proposition** reflects the benefits and costs created by the competitive offerings for collaborators and the reasons why collaborators might prefer competitive offerings to those created by the company. The key questions here are: *What benefits and costs do the competitive offerings create for collaborators? What is the primary reason why collaborators might prefer a competitive offering to the company offering?*

- The **attributes of the competitive offerings** involve their product, service, brand, price, incentives, communication, and distribution components. The key questions here are: *What are the product, service, brand, price, incentives, communication, and distribution aspects of the competitive offerings? How do the attributes of the competitive offerings create collaborator value?*

The Collaborator Value Proposition

The collaborator value proposition defines the worth of an offering to company collaborators. The collaborator value proposition is identified by the *collaborator value equation*, the *competitive advantage* of the company's offering, and the *reason* why collaborators would choose the company's offering.

- The **collaborator value equation** identifies the benefits and costs created by the offering on two value dimensions: monetary and strategic. The key question here is: *What monetary and strategic benefits and costs does the offering create for collaborators?*

- The **competitive advantage** reflects the ability of the company's offering to address collaborators' goals better than the alternative options. The key questions here are: *Why should collaborators choose to partner with the company instead of using alternative means to achieve their goals? What are the points of dominance, points of parity, and points of compromise of the company's offering relative to the competitive offerings?*

- The **reason to choose** identifies the key factor(s) that would motivate collaborators to partner with the company. The key questions here are: *What is the primary reason for collaborators to partner with the company? How would collaborators justify choosing the company's offering?*

Collaborator Offering

The collaborator offering represents the collaborator aspect of the market offering. It is defined by the seven attributes that delineate the company's offering and the value that each of these attributes creates for collaborators. The key questions here are: *What are the key features of the product, service, brand, price, and incentives the company offers to its collaborators? How will the offering be communicated to collaborators? How will the offering be delivered to collaborators? How will different attributes of the offering create collaborator value?*

The Company Value Map

The company value map outlines the ways in which the offering can enable the company to achieve its goals better than it can with alternative options. The company value map aims to address the question:

How does the offering create superior value for the company?

The company value map has a structure similar to the customer and collaborator value maps and consists of four building blocks: *the company, the alternative options, the company value proposition*, and *the company offering*. The core components of the company value map are shown in the figure below and are outlined in more detail in the following sections.

The Company Value Map

Company		Company Offering	
Company profile — What entity is managing the offering? What are its key resources?		**Product** — What are the features of the product that the company offers to target customers and collaborators?	
Company goals — What goal does the company aim to fulfill with this offering?		**Service** — What are the features of the service that the company offers to target customers and collaborators?	
Alternative Options		**Brand** — What are the features of the offering's brand?	
Key alternatives — What alternative options can fulfill the same company goal?		**Price** — What is the offering's price for target customers and collaborators?	
Value proposition — What value do these options create for the company?		**Incentives** — What incentives does the offering provide to target customers and collaborators?	
Option attributes — What are the key aspects of the alternative options?		**Communication** — How will target customers and collaborators become aware of the company's offering?	
Company Value		**Distribution** — How will the offering be delivered to target customers and collaborators?	
Reason to choose — What value does the offering create for target customers? Why would customers choose this offering?			

The Company

The company is the entity in charge of the offering. The company is defined by two factors: the company *profile* and the *goals* that the company aims to achieve with the offering.

- The **company profile** outlines the key aspects of the entity in charge of the offering. The key questions here are: *What entity is in charge of the offering? What resources does the company have to fulfill the identified need of the target customers?*

- **Company goals** are the strategic and monetary outcomes that the company aims to achieve with the offering. The key question here is: *What monetary and strategic goals is the company pursuing by creating the offering?*

Alternative Options

From a company's perspective, alternative options are the different means that could enable the company to achieve its goals. The alternative options are identified by the *key alternatives*, their *value proposition* for the company, and their *attributes*.

- **Key alternatives** are the other options that compete with the focal offering for the company's resources. The key questions here are: *What is the company currently doing to achieve its goals? What alternative offerings could enable the company to achieve its goals? What would the company give up if it chooses to invest in the focal offering?*

- The **value proposition of the alternative options** reflects the benefits and costs created by the options the company could pursue instead of investing in the focal offering. The key questions here are: *What benefits and costs do the alternative options create for the company? What is the primary reason why the company would choose to invest resources in the alternative options?*

- The **attributes of the alternative options** are the characteristics of the options that the company could pursue instead of investing in the focal offering. The key questions here are: *What are the product, service, brand, price, incentives, communication, and distribution aspects of the alternative options? How do the attributes of the alternative options create company value?*

The Company Value Proposition

The company value proposition defines the worth of an offering for the company stakeholders. The company value proposition is identified by the *company value equation*, the *relative advantage* of the company's offering over the alternative options, and the *reason* why the company would choose to invest in this offering.

- The **company value equation** reflects the benefits and costs created by the offering on the two dimensions of company value: monetary and strategic. The key questions here are: *What monetary and strategic benefits and costs does the offering create for the company? What is this offering's profit formula?*

- The **relative advantage** reflects the focal offering's ability to address the company's goals better than the alternative options. The key questions here are: *Why* *should the company choose to invest resources in the focal offering instead of using alternative means to achieve its goals? What are the points of dominance, points of parity, and points of compromise of the focal offering relative to the alternative options?*

- The **reason to choose** is the key factor(s) that would motivate the company to invest in this offering. The key questions here are: *What is the primary reason for the company to pursue this offering? How would the company management justify choosing this offering?*

The Company Offering

The company offering represents the company aspect of the market offering. It is defined by the seven attributes — product, service, brand, price, incentives, communication, and distribution — that delineate the offering and the value that each of these attributes creates for the company. The key questions here are: *What are the key features of the product, service, brand, price, and incentives the company offers to its customers and collaborators? How will the offering be communicated to target customers and collaborators? How will the offering be delivered to target customers and collaborators? How will different attributes of the offering create company value?*

BUSINESS MODEL ARCHETYPES

*The marble not yet carved can hold the form
of every thought the greatest artist has.*
— Michelangelo, Italian sculptor and painter

Business models vary across companies and industries. Despite these differences, business models have common, recurring themes. These recurring themes — referred to as archetypes — reflect the particular ways in which companies create market value. Based on their level of generality, there are two types of business model archetypes. *Strategic archetypes* focus on creating market value without explicitly dealing with the tactical aspects of the company offering. In contrast, *tactical archetypes* focus on how different attributes of the offering — product, service, brand, price, incentives, communication, and distribution — create market value.

Strategic Business Model Archetypes

From a strategic standpoint, business models vary based on the types of entities involved and the value relationships among these entities. Specifically, there are four common types of business models: *business-to-consumer (B2C)*, *business-to-business (B2B)*, *business-to-business-to-consumer (B2B2C)*, and *consumer-to-consumer (C2C)*.

Business-to-Consumer (B2C) Model

B2C business models involve scenarios in which a company creates offerings aimed at individuals who are typically the end users of these offerings. This model is common for consumer packaged goods companies such as Procter & Gamble, Unilever, and Nestlé, as well as for consumer-focused service companies such as retail banks, hotels, and airlines. The B2C model also includes collaborators — suppliers, distributors, and co-developers — that work with the company to create value for consumers.

Business-to-Consumer (B2C) Model

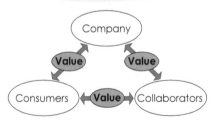

Business-to-Business (B2B) Model

The B2B model is similar to the B2C model, with the key difference that customers are business entities rather than consumers. B2B business models involve scenarios in which a company—a manufacturer or service provider—and its collaborators create offerings aimed at businesses that are the end users of these offerings. This model is common for businesses that offer products and services to fulfill the needs of other businesses.

Business-to-Business (B2B) Model

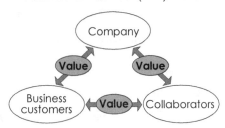

Business to Business to Consumer (B2B2C) Model

The B2B2C model combines B2B and B2C models, and describes a scenario in which a company, working with its collaborators, delivers its offering to another business entity, which, in turn, delivers it to end users (consumers). The B2B2C model is common for manufacturers and service providers distributing their offerings through intermediaries (dealers, wholesalers, retailers) as well as businesses producing ingredients for offerings created by other companies (Intel). Similar to B2C and B2B, the B2B2C model also involves collaborators that work with the company and its business customers to create value for the end users.

Business-to-Business-to-Consumer (B2B2C) Business Model

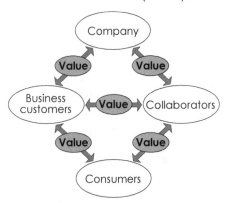

Customer to Customer (C2C) Model

The C2C model describes scenarios in which a company facilitates interactions between individual customers. These interactions can involve communications (Facebook, LinkedIn, Instagram, Twitter), monetary transactions (eBay, PayPal, Square), and services (Uber, Airbnb, Freelancer). The C2C model can be viewed as a specific instance of a B2C model in which the company and its collaborators create value for their customers by providing a platform that enables customer-to-customer interactions.

Customer-to-Customer (C2C) Model

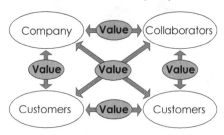

Tactical Business Model Archetypes

From a tactical standpoint, business models vary in the ways the offering attributes—product, service, brand, price, incentives, communication, and distribution—work together to create market value. Popular tactical business model archetypes include the *rent* model, the *software-as-a-service* model, the *crowdsourcing* model, the *licensing* model, the *private-label* model, the *ingredient-branding* model, the *subscription* model, the *product-service-bundle* model, the *razor-and-blades* model, the *freemium* model, the *loss-leader* model, the *fee-for-service* model, the *buy-one-get-one* model, the *one-for-one* model, the *market-penetration* model, the *market-skimming* model, the *dynamic-pricing* model, the *surge-pricing* model, the *auction* model, the *reverse-pricing* model, the *pay-what-you-want* model, the *free-trial* model, the *omni-channel distribution* model, the *direct-to-consumer* model, the *online-to-offline* model, the *store-within-a-store* model, the *push* model, the *pull* model, and the *franchise* model.

Rent Model

The rent model offers a company's products as a service. For example, Netflix offers a movie-streaming and DVD-rental service that aims to replace product (movie) ownership; music-streaming services iTunes, Pandora, and Spotify aim to replace compact disk ownership; Zipcar, Lyft, and Uber offer rental and transportation services that aim to replace car ownership; and luxury rental companies like Rent the Runway aim to replace ownership of designer apparel and accessories.

Rent Model

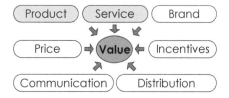

Software-as-a-Service Model

The software-as-a-service (SaaS) model is a software-specific version of the rent model. The SaaS model involves renting (licensing) a company's software to customers rather than selling it as a free-standing product. SaaS has gained popularity with the advance of cloud computing, with a growing number of companies including Microsoft, SAP, Adobe, and Salesforce.com switching to service-based offerings.

Software-as-a-Service Model

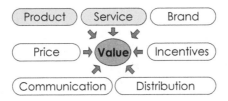

Crowdsourcing Model

The crowdsourcing model seeks input into developing new products and services from large groups of individuals rather than internally developing all aspects of the new offering. For example, unlike the traditional approach of using a professional editorial team for content development, Wikipedia content is developed by individuals unrelated to the company. Crowdsourcing has been extensively used by a variety of innovation-driven companies, ranging from high-tech powerhouses Apple, Google, and Microsoft to luxury giants Louis Vuitton, Hermès, and Tiffany & Co.

Crowdsourcing Model

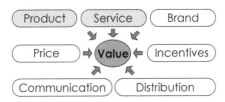

Licensing Model

The licensing model involves lending the rights to legally protected attributes of an offering to an entity that is different from the legal owner of these rights. Licensing can involve granting the rights to a patent, a copyright, a trade secret, or a trademark. For example, Disney, Calvin Klein, Mattel, and Lacoste license other entities to use their brands.

Licensing Model

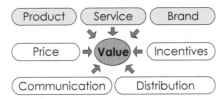

Ingredient-Branding Model

The ingredient-branding model involves creating a brand for a product or service that is a component of another offering. One of the most prominent examples of ingredient branding is Intel, which has managed to build customer loyalty for a product that most buyers never see or touch. Other prominent examples include Gore-Tex and Teflon coating technologies, as well as sugar substitutes Splenda and NutraSweet. Ingredient branding stands out from traditional branding in that the branded ingredient is an integral part of another offering and is typically not used as a stand-alone product or service (sugar substitutes are one of the few exceptions).

Ingredient-Branding Model

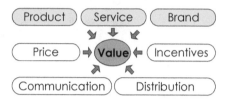

Private-Label Model

The private-label model involves brands created by retailers in order to differentiate themselves from the competition, build a loyal customer base, and increase profit margins. Private labels typically are not advertised outside of the specific retail channel and are often priced lower than the leading brands. To illustrate, Bayer aspirin, the leading global brand, is available across a variety of distribution channels and promoted through diverse communication channels, whereas Kirkland Signature aspirin, a private label, is available only through Costco, is not promoted outside of Costco, and is offered at a lower price point.

Private-Label Model

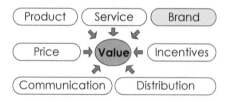

Subscription Model

The subscription model provides customers with the company's products and services on a recurring basis rather than selling them one at a time. The subscription typically involves a price discount compared to purchasing the same products and services individually. The subscription model is popular in a number of industries, including print and digital media, retail, and social and sport clubs.

Subscription Model

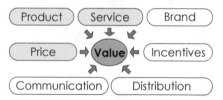

Razor-and-Blades Model

The razor-and-blades model involves setting a low price for one product (or giving it away for free) to facilitate sales of a complementary product. For example, Gillette often prices its razors near cost and even gives them away in order to encourage new customers to adopt its shaving system and start purchasing its higher margin cartridges. Likewise, HP and Samsung set a relatively low price (compared to development and production costs) for its printers and a relatively high price for the print cartridges.

Razor-and-Blades Model

Product-Service-Bundle Model

The product-service-bundle model is similar to the razor-and-blades model in that it is a two-part offering with one of the components priced to subsidize the other. Unlike the razor-and-blades model, which involves products that are uniquely compatible and which typically does not involve a long-term contract, the product-service-bundle model combines products with services and typically requires a long-term service contract. For example, a mobile phone company might set a low price on handsets (or give them away) and charge a higher price for its services in order to offset the cost of the handsets.

Product-Service-Bundle Model

Freemium Model

The freemium model involves a two-tier offering in which the basic version of the product or service is offered for free while giving the customer an option to upgrade to a fully functional paid version. The freemium model is commonly used to promote a new offering by enabling consumers to experience the offering at no cost. For example, Amazon.com (Kindle), Dropbox, Hulu, and Pandora make available both a free basic version of their offerings as well as a paid, fully functional (unrestricted) version. The freemium model is similar to the razor-and-blades and the product-service-bundle models in that it involves two-part pricing but differs in that both components have similar core functionality, with one component a premium version of the other.

Freemium Model

Offering A (free)   Offering B (premium)

Loss-Leader Model

The loss-leader model involves pricing one offering near or below cost in order to stimulate demand for another offering. For example, a retailer might price a popular item at a loss in order to generate store traffic and thus recoup the loss (or lost profit) on the low-priced item. The loss-leader model is similar to the razor-and-blades, product-service-bundle, and freemium models in that it involves product-line pricing but differs in that the loss leader usually is not functionally related to the offering(s) it benefits.

Loss-Leader Model

Offering A (loss leader)   Offering B (profit center)

Fee-for-Service Model

The fee-for-service model involves offering services on an à-la-carte basis rather than as a bundle. Under the fee-for-service model, customers can choose which services to use and pay for them individually rather than as a package. For example, a health care provider might charge a fee for each service performed (office visit, test, or procedure) instead of offering comprehensive service coverage.

Fee-for-Service Model

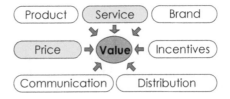

Buy-One-Get-One Model

The buy-one-get-one (BOGO) model involves offering a free item as an incentive to purchase the promoted item. The BOGO approach is particularly relevant when a company aims to rapidly increase sales volume (for example, in order to reduce inventory). A variation of the BOGO approach involves offering a heavily discounted (rather than free) item with the purchase of a regularly priced one (buy one, get one half off).

Buy-One-Get-One Model

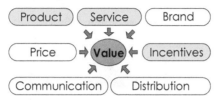

One-for-One Model

The one-for-one model (also referred to as buy-one-give-one) is a variation of the buy-one-get-one (BOGO) model. However, instead of giving customers a free item with every item purchased, a company either donates the second item or makes a monetary donation to have the second item distributed for free to those in need. For example, Toms donates a pair of shoes for every pair purchased, Soapbox Soaps provides a bar of soap to a person in need for every product sold, and Warby Parker donates money to have a pair of prescription eyeglasses given to a low-income consumer for every pair of eyeglasses sold.

One-for-One Model

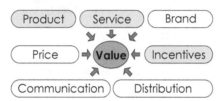

Market-Penetration Model

The market-penetration model involves a low pricing strategy in which the company aims to meet its profit goals by generating high sales volume, albeit at low profit margins. For example, a software developer might price an app at $.99 in order to generate market demand and make money on volume rather than margins.

Market-Penetration Model

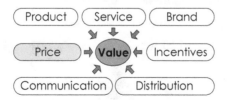

Market-Skimming Model

The market-skimming model involves a premium-pricing strategy in which the company aims to meet its profit goals by generating a high profit margin while sacrificing some sales volume. With its focus on margins rather than volume, the market-skimming model has a philosophy that is diametrically opposite to the market-penetration model. For example, Patek Philippe, a Swiss watch manufacturer, sells most of its watches at prices starting at $20,000 and reaching into seven figures, making money on margins rather than volume.

Market-Skimming Model

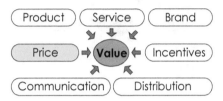

Dynamic-Pricing Model

The dynamic-pricing model involves varying prices based on factors such as supply and demand, competitive offerings, and the overall market environment. Unlike the traditional approach, in which prices are relatively stable and demand is stimulated by incentives, dynamic pricing typically involves a range of prices that change frequently to adapt to market conditions. Dynamic pricing is a common practice in the hospitality, travel, and energy industries.

Dynamic-Pricing Model

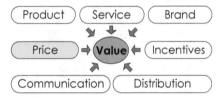

Surge-Pricing Model

The surge-pricing model is a specific instance of dynamic pricing. The difference is that surge pricing involves premium pricing (such as using a price multiplier), whereas dynamic pricing can involve price fluctuations in both directions (price increases as well as price decreases). The surge-pricing model has been most prominently used by Uber, which charges surge rates as a multiplier of the base fare during periods of high demand.

Surge-Pricing Model

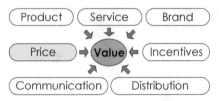

Auction Model

The auction model involves pricing that is determined by buyers who compete with one another to purchase a particular item. The auction model is commonly used for unique items such as art, antiquities, and rare artifacts; for items that must be sold within a given time frame; and when sellers are willing to let the market determine the price of the items being sold. Companies that use auction pricing include fine art auction houses Christie's and Sotheby's and online auctioneers eBay and Taobao.

Auction Model

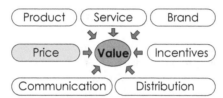

Reverse-Pricing Model

The reverse-pricing model (also referred to as name-your-own-price model) is similar to auction pricing in that buyers have to place a bid for the item they wish to acquire. Unlike auctions, where buyers directly compete with one another, in reverse pricing buyers submit their bids to the company, which then decides how many and which bids to accept. Companies utilizing reverse pricing include Priceline.com, Groupon, and eBay.

Reverse-Pricing Model

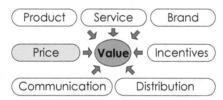

Pay-What-You-Want Model

The pay-what-you-want model is similar to reverse pricing in that buyers set the purchase price of a given item. The key difference is that in reverse pricing the seller has the ability to reject bids that do not meet certain criteria, such as minimum purchase price or volume. In contrast, in the pay-what-you-want approach the seller does not control the price set by the buyer. The pay-what-you-want model is used primarily when the marginal costs of the offering are low, such as in the case of digital content: information, music, and video. The pay-what-you-want model is also used when the average price paid by consumers is likely to be higher than the cost of the offering, and thus has the potential to generate additional sales while minimizing the risk of financial loss.

Pay-What-You-Want-Price Model

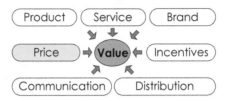

Free-Trial Model

The free-trial model involves providing target customers with an option to experience the offering at no cost. The free-trial model is popular with companies in a variety of industries that include food manufacturers, pharmaceutical companies, software developers, and content providers (news, music, video). The free-trial model is particularly common in new product introduction because it reduces customer risk of trying a new offering. Contrary to the popular view of free trials as an incentive, they are actually a form of communication—a means for the company to inform target customers about the benefits of its offering (by letting them experience the offering rather than by merely advertising its benefits).

Free-Trial Model

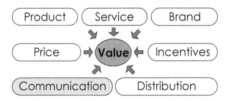

Omni-Channel Distribution Model

The omni-channel distribution model combines offline (brick and mortar) and online retail outlets. For example, most brick-and-mortar retailers such as Best Buy, Walmart, and Target have created an online division to take advantage of the growth of online retailing. In addition to brick-and-mortar retailers going online, the omni-channel model has been adopted by online retailers such as Amazon.com, cosmetics shop Birchbox, and fashion retailer Bonobos to establish a physical market presence.

Omni-Channel Distribution Model

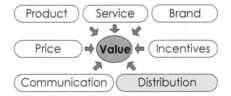

Direct-to-Consumer Model

The direct-to-consumer model streamlines the distribution channel by eliminating the intermediaries—dealers, wholesalers, brokers, and agents—between the manufacturer or service provider and the offering's end users. Amazon, Bonobos, Dollar Shave Club, and Warby Parker exemplify the direct-to-consumer model.

Direct-to-Consumer Model

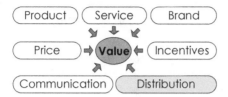

Online-to-Offline Model

The online-to-offline (O2O) business model aims to draw potential buyers from the online space to physical retail outlets. The O2O model is very similar to traditional online advertising, with the key difference that instead of enticing customers who are already online to visit an online outlet, it encourages customers to leave the online space and visit a brick-and-mortar retailer.

Online-to-Offline Model

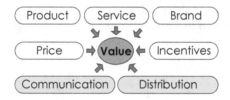

Store-within-a-Store Model

The store-within-a-store (also referred to as shop-in-shop) model involves a retailer allocating part of its retail space to a branded manufacturer. For example, department stores such as Neiman Marcus, Macy's, and Nordstrom enable manufacturers of lifestyle brands such as Armani, Ralph Lauren, and Nautica to create a proprietary "brand oasis" that conveys the essence of their brands and enables them to better manage the overall customer experience. In addition to lifestyle apparel and cosmetics brands, the store-within-a-store concept is also popular among technology firms that aim to strengthen their brands. To illustrate, Best Buy provides companies like Microsoft, Apple, and Samsung with dedicated retail space that enables these companies to display the full array of their products and services and showcase their functionality.

Store-within-a-Store Model

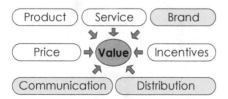

Push Model

The push model involves promoting an offering to a company's channel partners—distributors, retailers, and the sales force—so that they promote the company's offering(s) to target customers. For example, a manufacturer can offer incentives to retailers to motivate them to push a company's products to target customers, thus generating demand for these products.

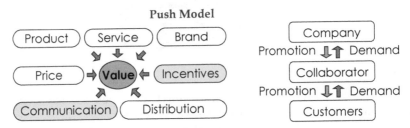

Push Model

Pull Model

The pull model involves promoting an offering directly to the company's customers in order to create demand for the company's offering(s). For example, a manufacturer can promote its products by advertising them directly to consumers and offer coupons, rebates, and price discounts, thus enticing consumers to pull the product from retailers' shelves.

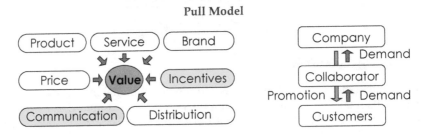

Pull Model

Franchise Model

The franchise model offers another party access to the resources needed to operate an already established business model. Under the franchise model, franchisors specify the products, services, and brands to be offered; grant intellectual property rights to these products, services, and brands; and offer logistical, financial, and marketing support for the franchisee operations. Examples of franchise business models include McDonald's, Coca-Cola, Subway, Dunkin' Donuts, Pizza Hut, Taco Bell, and KFC.

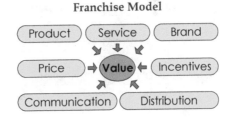

Franchise Model

2

BUSINESS MODEL GENERATION

THE PATH TO SUCCESS

The real voyage of discovery consists not in seeking new landscapes, but in having new eyes.
— Marcel Proust, French writer

Business success does not just happen; it is the result of a series of trials and errors that ultimately lead to a viable market offering. Companies vary in the way they create their business models: Some follow a systematic approach and others stumble on an effective way to address an unmet market need. Although there is no unique path to business model development, sustainable business models share a number of common elements that determine their market success. These common drivers of market success are outlined below.

Innovation and Design Thinking

The concept of design thinking was born as an alternative to the view of design as a downstream aspect of the product development process, in which the role of designers is limited to making an already developed idea or product more attractive to customers. In contrast, design thinking asserts that designers should play a central role not only in optimizing an already developed idea or product but also should actively participate in creating these ideas and products.

The concept of design thinking has been advanced by David Kelley and Tim Brown from the global design powerhouse IDEO, who define design thinking as "a discipline that uses the designer's sensibility and methods to match people's needs with an offering that is technologically feasible and that a viable business strategy can convert into customer value and market opportunity." Design thinking is an approach to new product development that focuses on the overall customer experience rather than only on functional product performance. Design thinking calls for innovation powered by a thorough understanding of what people want and need in their lives and what they like and dislike about the way particular products are made, packaged, marketed, sold, and supported.[2]

Initially used in reference to product design, the concept of design thinking is now also used in customer-centric product development, where idea discovery and product development go hand in hand to pair customers' needs with technologically feasible solutions. In this broader sense, design thinking goes beyond aesthetics: It aims to identify a customer need that can serve as a basis for creating customer benefits and value for the company.

An important aspect of design thinking is *prototyping*—creating a simple version of the product to facilitate development of the underlying idea. The importance of prototyping in design thinking is captured in the MIT Media Lab credo, "Demo or Die," meaning that transforming an idea into a meaningful product is an essential component of product development and that ideas have little value unless they are expressed in a tangible form.

Design thinking is an important aspect of business model development because it articulates a set of principles that are fundamental to creating market value and achieving business success—including a focus on understanding the functional and psychological aspects of customer needs, relying on prototyping as a key means of product development, and regarding (small and early) failures as an opportunity for improvement and innovation.

The Stage-Gate Approach to Business Model Development

Business model development is not a one-shot deal. It is an ongoing process of formulating, testing, realigning, and pivoting in which the company identifies an optimal way to create market value. Business model development typically starts with a rough idea that evolves into a clearly defined vision. The process of business model development can be represented as a sequence of actions (stages) separated by hurdles (gates) that a company must overcome. The stage-gate approach is a process of designing and validating the business model in a way that minimizes risk and optimizes allocation of the company's resources.

A streamlined version of the stage-gate approach to business model development involves four key stages—*idea discovery, concept development, business model design,* and *business model implementation*—separated by hurdles that aim to validate the actions taken in the previous step.

The Stage-Gate Approach to Business Model Development

- **Idea discovery.** Business model development starts with the discovery of an idea that uncovers an unmet market need and a novel way to address this need. The idea discovery is followed by an assessment of the soundness of the idea and validation of its key assumptions.

- **Concept development.** The validated idea is further refined and fleshed out to create an initial version (prototype) of the offering. The developed concept is validated with respect to its technological feasibility and its potential to fulfill the identified customer need.

- **Business model design.** The validated concept evolves into a business model that articulates the company's target market, defines the value created and captured by the company in this market, and delineates the key aspects of the company's offering. The business model is validated with respect to its ability to fulfill the identified customer need in a way that creates value for the company and its collaborators.

- **Business model implementation.** The validated business model is deployed in the market — a process that involves developing the resources needed to create the offering, development of the actual offering, deployment of this offering in selected markets, and market expansion that makes the offering available across the entire target market.

The above four steps are a stylized version of the process of developing a business model. On many occasions, business model development might not follow a predefined series of orderly, well-articulated steps but, instead, might comprise a number of interrelated activities that do not follow the linear architecture of the stage-gate approach outlined here. Nevertheless, even when the individual steps are not clearly defined, business model development typically follows the stage-gate approach presented in this book.

Business Model Development as an Iterative Process

Business model development is not a linear process in which the initial idea naturally evolves into a successful market offering. Rather, it is an *iterative process* of discovering a novel idea and translating this idea into a sustainable business model. Business model development involves a series of iterations — *realignments* and *pivots* — aimed at developing a successful market offering.

- **Realignments** are relatively minor changes to an idea, concept, or business model that do not substantially alter the core value proposition. Realignment typically involves making tactical changes and modifying certain aspects of the offering without changing its target customers and its value proposition.

- **Pivots** are major changes that involve going back to the drawing board and modifying some (or all) of the key aspects of the initial idea, concept, or business model. Pivoting typically includes a change in a company's strategy — target customers and value proposition — followed by a change in its tactics. Pivots are *strategic inflection points* that change the fundamentals of the business model.

Business Model Iterations

Realignment
Adjusting the tactics
without changing the
underlying strategy

Pivot
Changing both
the strategy and
the tactics

One of the most prominent examples of pivoting is that of *The Point*, a social media company designed to facilitate fundraising. The problem The Point was trying to solve was that people were reluctant to donate because of concerns about the social relevance of the cause and the reputation of the fundraising organization. To address these concerns, the company enabled the fundraiser to set a tipping point — a certain amount of money or number of participants needed for the program to be activated. The actual donations were not collected until the set goal was met, thus assuring potential donors that they were contributing to a socially relevant cause supported by many other donors.

Despite being a promising idea that addressed what appeared to be a valid customer concern, The Point did not gain much traction with its target audience. There was one bright spot though: a growing number of consumers used the website to find lower prices and sales, and the most successful campaigns were those that enabled consumers to combine their buying power to save money.

In a now classic pivot, The Point redefined its entire business model to focus on business owners rather than fundraisers and created an entirely new value proposition, enabling vendors to set a tipping point that would activate a promotional offer. Participating vendors could benefit from the new business generated by the promotional offer without having to pay anything if their offer did not generate sufficient customer demand. The revised value proposition for customers — lower prices — was straightforward and particularly appealing in the midst of an economic crisis, when many consumers were financially strained. Pivoting to redefine its business model turned the struggling social media fundraising company *The Point* into *Groupon*, the multibillion-dollar deal-of-the-day company.

Business Model Design as a Process of Creating Market Value

The ultimate goal of the business model is to create market value. To this end, the initial idea undergoes a number of pivots and realignments, resulting in a sustainable business model. Pivots and realignments in designing the company's offering are guided by three key principles: *desirability*, *feasibility*, and *viability*:

- Desirability reflects the degree to which target customers find the offering attractive. Because customer value is a function of benefits and costs, an offering's desirability might be hindered by its inability to deliver the benefits sought by customers and/or by the high costs — money, time, and effort — associated with the offering. For example, Crystal Pepsi, a clear, caffeine-free alternative to regular colas, failed despite a massive promotional campaign because consumers did not find the concept of clear cola appealing. Another example of a product that failed to meet consumer desirability criteria was Lisa — a personal computer designed by Apple in the early 1980s — which had a $10,000 price tag that far exceeded customers' willingness to pay for the device.

- Feasibility reflects the degree to which the company has the ability to build an offering that has the functionality desired by customers. Feasibility is a function of current technologies and the company's ability to utilize these technologies. For example, long-range electric cars are currently not feasible because of limited battery capacity. Ultimate examples of projects that are not considered feasible are a perpetual motion machine and a time machine.

- Viability reflects the degree to which an offering is capable of creating value for the company. The viability of an offering from a for-profit perspective is reflected in its ability to generate profits. Viability is typically a function of the expected revenue streams from an offering and its cost structure. The inability to align revenues and costs is often a precursor of market failure. For example, despite its high-profile promotional campaign and a widely recognized public presence, online pet supply retailer Pets.com lost money on most of its sales and ultimately went out of business due to its weak fundamentals.

Because a company's success is driven by the desirability, feasibility, and viability of its offerings, the sustainability of the business model is determined by the answers to the following three sets of questions:

Is the offering desirable? Does it create value for target customers?

Is the offering feasible? Can it actually be built as planned?

Is the offering viable? Does it create value for the company managing it?

The desirability, feasibility, and viability aspects of the offering are typically related. An offering that is undesirable to customers would likely not prove to be viable because it would not generate sufficient customer demand to create value for the company. In the same vein, an offering that is not technologically feasible would also fail the desirability test because the offering that can actually be built would not fulfill customer needs.

Consider the Newton—the personal digital assistant created by Apple in the early 1990s. It had a variety of novel features, including a touchscreen for entering data, an appointment calendar, a to-do list, an address book, a calculator, and note-taking capability. Despite the plethora of features, Newton's high price ($700) and glitchy handwriting recognition software handicapped its market performance. As a result, the Newton faded away several years after introduction, unable to generate sufficient interest among potential buyers.

Newton's failure stemmed from its lack of desirability (high price and inferior performance), which was partially driven by the low feasibility of the project (high development cost and nascent handwriting recognition technology). The low desirability and feasibility, in turn, reduced the potential of the Newton to create value for Apple, rendering the project non-viable from the company's perspective.

In the same vein, Iridium—the multibillion-dollar venture led by Motorola—promised to revolutionize mobile communications by offering international business travelers one number, one phone, one bill anywhere on the planet. Iridium's concept, however, was not feasible because of the technological constraints involved in designing a small satellite phone that ensured reliable connection anywhere in the world. The high cost of the project—building a constellation of 77 satellites capable of transferring calls across different terrestrial networks—coupled with the alternative means of communication available to customers dramatically limited its viability as a profitable business enterprise.

To recoup its investment and generate profits, Iridium had to set an exorbitantly high price for its offering, with handsets priced at around $3,000 and usage rates ranging between $3 and $8 per minute. Customers, however, did not see the value in having a very expensive, bulky phone that featured a short battery life, an unreliable connection, and spotty service. As a result, after more than a decade of development and burning through $5 billion in capital from investors, Iridium filed for bankruptcy less than a year following its market launch.

As was the case with the Newton, Iridium's failure stemmed from the fact that the project was not a feasible substitute for terrestrial wireless communications and had little appeal for its target customer—the international business traveler. Lacking customer desirability, Iridium was unable to generate the revenues needed to recoup its investment and sustain the project, and ultimately was forced to fold its operations.

Even though the Newton and Iridium failed, they were the precursors of successful offerings that pivoted their original business models and created viable offerings. The Newton was the precursor of the Palm Pilot—a highly successful personal digital assistant that offered the basic functionality of the Newton in a much more reliable fashion and at a lower price. The Palm Pilot was then eclipsed by the iPhone, which expanded its functionality by improving its interface and adding the ability to communicate by voice, text, and email.

Likewise, following Iridium's bankruptcy, its assets were acquired by a group of investors who repositioned the company's offering by broadening its target market to include wealthy consumers, as well as maritime, exploration, military, and business-to-business customers; by improving the technology; and by changing the pricing structure. Ten years later, the new Iridium went public after several years of profitable growth.

IDEA DISCOVERY

An innovation will get traction only if it helps people get something that they're already doing in their lives done better.
—Clayton Christensen, author of *The Innovator's Dilemma*

Innovation is the key to developing a viable business model. Innovation is not limited to the development of new products. It can involve a new technology (3-D printing), a new service (Uber), a new approach to building a brand (Warby Parker), a new pricing mechanism (Priceline.com), a new approach to manage incentives (Groupon), a new means of communication (Facebook), or a novel distribution method (Amazon.com). Innovative business models change the way markets operate by discovering new ways to create market value, disrupting existing business models and driving companies that fail to adapt into oblivion.

Innovation begins with the discovery of an idea that identifies an unmet market need and a novel way to address this need. Based on the discovery process, there are two basic ways in which business ideas are born: top down and bottom up.

Top-Down Idea Discovery

Top-down idea discovery starts with identifying a market opportunity and is followed by an invention designed to address this opportunity. When exploring a market opportunity, the company seeks to identify an important problem faced by its potential customers that it can solve better than the available alternatives can. Accordingly, top-down idea discovery starts with a market analysis that aims to identify an unmet need that the company can fulfill better than the competition.

Top-Down (Market-Driven) Idea Discovery

Top-down idea discovery has resulted in a number of successful products designed to seize an identified market opportunity:

Apple's iPod addressed the need for a user-friendly device that enables people to carry their favorite music with them.

Apple's iPhone addressed the need for a user-friendly device that combines the functionality of a mobile phone, a personal digital assistant, a music player, and a camera.

Apple's iPad addressed the need for a portable, user-friendly mobile device that offers enhanced iPhone functionality with a larger display.

Procter & Gamble designed *Swiffer* to address the need for a cleaning tool that is more effective than a mop and cuts down on cleaning time.

Herman Miller designed the *Aeron* chair to address the need for an office chair that is both comfortable and stylish.

Dyson designed its iconic vacuum cleaner to address the need for a vacuum that does not lose suction with usage.

Tesla designed its S-class sedan to address the need for an environmentally friendly, fuel-efficient, premium car that is fast, spacious, and stylish.

Bottom-Up Idea Discovery

Bottom-up idea discovery starts with an invention, followed by identification of a market need that can be fulfilled by this invention. Unlike top-down idea discovery, the invention here is not driven by an identified market need but by technological innovation. In this context, the bottom-up approach to idea discovery is more often the province of scientists in research labs than managers in market research departments.

Bottom-Up (Invention-Driven) Idea Discovery

Bottom-up idea discovery has resulted in a number of successful products that stem from technological innovation:

Post-it Notes were discovered by a 3M chemist who created a very weak pressure-sensitive adhesive while trying to come up with a super strong adhesive for use in the aerospace industry.

Viagra was originally devised by the drug company Pfizer to treat angina, a heart condition that constricts the vessels that supply the heart with blood. Although not very effective in relaxing these blood vessels, Viagra became a multibillion-dollar erectile dysfunction drug.

Rogaine (minoxidil) — the popular over-the-counter drug for treating hair loss — was originally used to treat high blood pressure; however, patients taking drugs containing minoxidil began to notice increased hair growth on their balding scalps, as well as on other parts of their bodies.

Penicillin — an antibiotic used to combat bacterial infections — was discovered by Scottish biologist Alexander Fleming, who noticed that the fungus growing on dirty dishes had killed the staphylococci bacteria he was researching.

The *microwave* was discovered by a Raytheon engineer, who noticed that the chocolate bar in his pocket melted when he walked in front of a vacuum tube generating microwaves.

Velcro was discovered by a Swiss engineer who noticed on a hiking trip that the hooks in burrs clung to anything loop-shaped — in this particular case, his pants and his dog's fur.

Teflon — the nonstick coating commonly used in cookware and other applications — was discovered by a DuPont engineer who was searching for a better fluid for refrigerators.

Even though bottom-up idea discovery starts with an invention, to evolve into a successful market offering the invention must address a viable market opportunity. Novel technology per se is not a reason for developing a new offering. While new technologies are often an important factor, the key driver of market success is the company's ability to apply this technology to address an unmet market need. Idea discovery, whether top-down or bottom-up, should always be linked to the market value it creates.

To transform a technological invention into a viable business idea, the company must identify a problem that this invention can solve and the market value it can create. Therefore, even though successful business ideas can be born serendipitously from a technological invention, *the top-down approach is the preferred idea discovery method* in business model development. Because the success of an offering ultimately depends on its ability to deliver market value, by starting with identifying value-creation opportunities in the market, a company can increase its chances of developing an invention that will enjoy market success.

Idea Discovery as a Value-Creation Process

To create value, an offering must increase customers' well-being by fulfilling an unmet need. Based on the degree to which a given need has already been fulfilled by alternative means, customers' assessment of this need can be characterized as a *problem, indifference,* or *delight.*

- **Problem.** Customers perceive an important need as a problem when they are *unsatisfied* with the existing means to fulfill it. These customers recognize that they have a problem (an unmet need), are unhappy with the status quo (doing nothing), and actively seek a solution to fulfill their unmet need. For example, the iPhone addressed a problem faced by many consumers who had to carry multiple devices, such as a phone, an organizer, a music player, and a camera. Likewise, Dollar Shave Club addressed consumers' problem of having to pay more than $4 for a single shaving cartridge.

- **Indifference.** Customers are indifferent when they are *reasonably satisfied* with the current options and are willing to stay the course without changing their behavior. Even though their needs might not be perfectly met and better alternatives might be available, customers do not consider this as a problem and are not actively seeking better options. For example, even though Google's Nest learning thermostat can benefit its target customers, many consumers are satisfied with the available thermostats that do a reasonably good job of regulating the temperature in their residences. Likewise, even though ultra-high-definition TVs can lead to a better viewing experience, most consumers are reasonably satisfied with their high-definition TVs.

- **Delight.** Customers are delighted when they are *extremely satisfied* with the current means of fulfilling a given need, believe that this need has been fully addressed, and tend to ignore alternative solutions. For example, Amazon's goal of meeting or exceeding customer expectations aims to delight its customers in order to deter them from exploring other options and create barriers for competitors considering entering its markets. In the same vein, Ritz-Carlton, Nordstrom, and Zappos (owned by Amazon) aim to earn customer loyalty by offering a level of service that delights their customers.

Based on customers' perception of a given need as a problem, indifference, or delight, there are two types of offerings: *problem-solving offerings* designed to address a customer problem by fulfilling a particular need and *experience-enhancing offerings* designed to improve on an existing solution to a given problem.

- **Problem-solving (must-have) offerings** provide a solution to an important unmet need that customers actively seek to fulfill. Because problem-solving ideas address an essential need that customers deem unresolved, these ideas are typically easy to communicate, and the offerings addressing these needs tend to be rapidly adopted by customers.

- **Experience-enhancing (nice-to-have) offerings** aim to improve on an offering that fulfills a given need reasonably well in order to provide customers with an even greater level of satisfaction. Because experience-enhancing offerings address a need that customers do not consider a problem, they are adopted at a much slower rate than problem-solving offerings.

Problem-solving and experience-enhancing offerings are often described in terms of customer pains and gains. Thus, problem-solving offerings are viewed as a way to *alleviate customer pain* by addressing a key source of dissatisfaction. In contrast, experience-enhancing offerings are described as a means to *produce customer gain* by improving on an already satisficing offering.

The distinction between problem-solving and experience-enhancing offerings is important because customers place greater value on offerings that solve recognized problems than on offerings that merely enhance their experience. Furthermore, compared to problem-solving offerings, communicating the benefits of experience-enhancing offerings typically calls for greater company resources and requires a significantly longer amount of time for customers to understand these benefits and recognize their value.

Problem-Solving and Experience-Enhancing Offerings

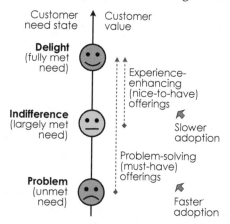

Many companies have failed to achieve their growth projections because of the erroneous belief that they could easily educate their customers and change their behavior to appreciate the benefits of offerings that did not address a problem (pain point) faced by these customers. For example, TiVo introduced the first digital video recorder at the turn of this century, expecting that it would gain rapid customer adoption and revolutionize the way consumers watched television. Revolutionize television viewing it did, but at a much slower rate than TiVo expected. The company ended up with a very small share of the digital video recording market after the competition moved in. What the TiVo team did not take into account is that consumers were reasonably satisfied with the way they watched TV and could not readily see the value of TiVo's offering. TiVo was perceived as a nice-to-have product; it was not a product customers felt they needed to have.

In the same vein, Fusion—Gillette's five-bladed razor—failed to gain traction with many consumers who were already very satisfied with Gillette's three-bladed Mach3. Likewise, many software companies including Microsoft, Adobe, and Intuit have had a difficult time inducing their customers to upgrade to the most recent versions of their offerings because the earlier versions are perfectly capable of fulfilling the needs of these customers. Facing the same predicament, the product upgrade cycle of many consumer electronics manufacturers including Apple, Samsung, and LG is slowing down because consumers are reasonably satisfied with their current offerings.

While offerings that marginally enhance customers' experience have been slow to gain market traction, offerings that provide a solution to an important problem faced by customers have taken the market by storm:

The *iPhone* offered customers the convenience of having a single device that could serve as a phone, a music player, a camera, and a contact manager, thus obviating the need to carry multiple devices.

Uber addressed customers' need for transportation by offering faster, more convenient, and more predictable service.

eBay offered a peer-to-peer trading platform connecting buyers with sellers, providing customers with a convenient way to dispose of unneeded items and acquire those they desire.

Facebook offered individuals a simple way to connect with others and exponentially broaden their social network.

The *Dollar Shave Club* offered a low-priced shaving system to address the pain point of many customers who were discontent with the prices of market leader Gillette.

Idea Validation

Idea validation assesses the soundness of the idea for the proposed offering and the validity of its key assumptions. Typically, idea validation involves a preliminary assessment of the *desirability* and *viability* of the offering—namely, whether an offering based on this idea is likely to fulfill an unmet customer need and do so in a way that benefits the company.

To validate an idea, a manager should ask the following questions: *What is the unmet customer need that is being addressed? Are there many customers who have this unmet need? Is this need perceived by customers as a problem that they actively seek to solve? Does the idea present a solution that will fulfill this need?*

In order to proceed to the next stage of concept development, the company must be able to answer the above questions. If these questions cannot be satisfactory addressed, the idea must be redefined.

Market Research Tools for Idea Discovery

Whether generated from the top down or bottom up, an idea must involve a sound understanding of the customer need it aims to address. Such an understanding is gained with market research.

Idea discovery and validation typically involve *exploratory research* that aims to identify unmet customer needs, formulate research questions (hypotheses), and generate ideas. Exploratory studies are typically used during the early stages of business model development to attain a general understanding of the market opportunity without quantifying the obtained insights or establishing causal relationships. Common exploratory methods involve *observation, personal interviews, focus group interviews*, and *activity-based studies*.

- Observation examines people's behavior in their natural environment to gain insights into their needs and the ways in which they address these needs. Many observational methods are derived from ethnography, a branch of anthropology that examines the sociocultural aspect of people's lives.

  Observation can involve monitoring people's physical behavior, including the way they go about evaluating, buying, and consuming products and services in order to fulfill their needs. Observation can also include monitoring people's online behavior, including the websites they visit, the content they focus on, and the information they share online.

- Personal interviews aim to explore in depth people's views, experiences, beliefs, and motivations in order to uncover their unmet needs, understand how they make decisions, and identify factors that influence their behavior. Based on the way they are conducted, interviews can be structured, unstructured, and semi-structured. *Structured interviews* are akin to questionnaires; all participants are asked the same predefined questions without being asked follow-up questions. *Unstructured interviews* do not follow a predetermined agenda and resemble a conversation in which respondents' answers determine the course of the interview. *Semi-structured interviews* combine features of both structured and unstructured interviews: They have an overarching narrative of questions but also allow follow-up questions when responses warrant further elaboration. Interviews can be conducted in person or indirectly, using questionnaires administered by mail or online.

- **Focus groups** are interviews conducted in groups rather than individually. Focus-group research involves engaging participants in a free-flowing discussion aimed at revealing their collective opinions on a given topic. Participants in these groups usually are the company's target customers, whose views, insights, and ideas the company wants to explore in an interactive social context.

  Focus groups are typically moderated by a professional facilitator whose role is to keep the discussion on point, explore potentially interesting ideas suggested by participants, and ensure that all participants have the opportunity to share their insights. The facilitator can also offer a meaningful interpretation of the discussion and relate it to the managerial questions the company aims to address.

  A key advantage of focus groups over one-on-one interviews is that they offer a broader range of insights, ideas, and opinions that stem from the socially interactive nature of the group discussion. Focus groups shed light on social dynamics, indicating how an individual's ideas are likely to be received by others. Focus groups are also faster and more cost-efficient than individual interviews. On the downside, group interactions can influence the discussion in a way that overemphasizes some ideas and overlooks others.

- **Activity-based studies** seek to gain insight into people's minds by asking them to perform specific tasks such as drawing a picture or arranging a series of images to create a narrative. These methods are rooted in the idea that people's beliefs, feelings, and motivations are better captured by actions rather than words.

  For example, study participants might be asked to collect pictures representing their thoughts and feelings related to a particular aspect of their lives. These pictures are then used as the basis for in-depth interviews to gain better insight into their individual beliefs, needs, and preferences.

  Because they offer an alternative approach to understanding target customers, activity-based studies are often used to complement observational studies and interviews.

CONCEPT DEVELOPMENT

I have not failed, I've just found 10,000 ways that won't work.
—Thomas Edison, American inventor and businessman

Concept development aims to refine and flesh out a potentially viable idea and create an initial version (prototype) of the company's offering. The ultimate goal of developing a concept of the offering prior to developing the actual offering is to improve the chances of market success. To this end, concept development involves evaluating people's response to the core benefit of the offering and molding the offering in a way that maximizes its market potential.

Concept Development as a Process of Managing Risk

One of the key challenges in new product development is managing the uncertainty associated with launching new offerings. Because uncertainty increases the risk of failure, minimizing risk is one of the key aspects of new product development.

The risk involved in new product development can be classified into one of two categories: *market risk* and *technology risk*.

- **Market risk** reflects the uncertainty associated with the market in which the company aims to compete. Market risk can involve some or all of the five Cs defining the market—customers, collaborators, company, competitors, and context. Thus, *customers* might not find the company's offering attractive or the customer segment might not be large enough to justify the development, production, promotion, and distribution of the offering. Likewise, the company's *collaborators*—suppliers, distributors, and codevelopers—might not find the offering sufficiently attractive to allocate the necessary support to ensure its success. The *company* might be unable to secure the resources necessary to develop and launch the offering. *Competitors* might gain pioneering advantage by being first to market, or they might emulate the company's technology to design a cheaper or a functionally superior offering. The offering's success could also be negatively influenced by changes in the market *context*, such as the availability of superior technologies, changing sociocultural trends, and new regulations involving product specifications, tariffs, taxes, and fees.

- **Technological risk** reflects the uncertainty associated with the technological feasibility of the new offering. For example, the desired product performance might not be achievable with currently available technologies, product design might not be compatible with the desired functionality, and product reliability might be compromised by the use of new, unproven technologies. Technological risk might also prolong the development of the new offering, which in turn can increase the risk of changes in the market conditions such as changes in customer needs and preferences, the emergence of new competitors, and the introduction of new regulations.

Concept development aims to reduce the market and technological risk by designing the offering in the most effective and resource-efficient way. To this end, concept development builds on the idea that the more complex the offering, the greater the resources — time, money, and effort — needed to bring it to market. Therefore, to minimize risk, concept development often involves creating a simplified version of the offering that requires a relatively small investment of resources to determine desirability, feasibility, and viability prior to investing additional resources in developing the final offering.

Prototyping

Concept development typically starts as a description of the core features of the offering and culminates in a scaled-down version, commonly referred to as a *prototype* (from the Greek πρωτότυπον, meaning *primitive form*). Developing a prototype aims to flesh out a potentially viable idea with a minimum investment of time, money, and effort. Because it is a scaled-down version of the company's offering, the prototype is typically limited to the key functionality of the offering (minimum viable offering) and addresses the most important aspect of the concept.

The development of a successful prototype follows five basic principles: *start small, stay focused, keep it simple, fail fast,* and *fail forward.*

- **Start small.** Some companies start out by trying to prototype a grand idea designed to address multiple, and at times unrelated, customer needs. The problem with this approach is that complex prototypes typically take time to develop and require considerable resources. The more complicated the idea, the more difficult and costly it is to design and test as a prototype, and the longer it takes to create. Therefore, regardless of the complexity of the underlying idea, the initial prototype must focus on fulfilling the most important customer need and build on this need rather than trying to implement all facets of the idea.

- **Stay focused.** Prototyping an idea typically opens a variety of possibilities for ways in which this can be done. Presented with such possibilities, a manager might lose focus and end up pursuing a variety of different, sometimes mutually exclusive, ideas. As a result, a relatively simple idea might evolve into an offering akin to a Swiss Army knife as it branches out into marginally related projects. Successful concept development calls for prototyping one idea at a time.

- **Keep it simple.** Starting with a simple idea and staying focused can still result in an overcomplicated prototype. This is because the desire for perfection can outweigh the primary purpose of a prototype — to develop a scaled-down version of the company's offering in order to minimize risk. Overcomplicating the prototype by including a variety of bells and whistles typically ends up being counterproductive and a waste of resources.

- **Fail fast.** Having failure as a goal might seem counterintuitive. After all, a company's ultimate goal is to succeed. Yet, when developing a prototype, failing is not necessarily a negative outcome. The goal of prototyping is not to avoid failing altogether but to fail fast, meaning failing early in the process before the company has committed significant resources to develop the offering. Failures enable the company to identify the aspects of its offering that do not work and improve them. In fact, failures are sometimes even more informative than successes. After confirming the core concept of the offering, a company might benefit from testing the boundaries of the offering's success by identifying cases in which the offering will fare poorly in the market. The key, however, is to fail early enough in the process so that the insight gained from the failure can be used to develop a better version of the offering.

- **Fail forward.** When developing new products, failure is inevitable. The key to managing failure is to fail forward by considering the failure as a learning experience that can help improve the offering. In the words of Thomas Edison: *Just because something doesn't do what you planned it to do doesn't mean it's useless.* Failing forward means analyzing the causes for failure and learning from mistakes in order to succeed in the future. A systematic approach to taking advantage of one's mistakes is the validated-learning method discussed in the next section.

The Minimum Viable Offering

Concept development often involves the creation of a *minimum viable offering* — a streamlined version of the offering that includes only the core features that are indispensable for fulfilling the focal customer need. The minimum viable offering is the simplest version of the offering that is able to deliver the primary benefit(s) sought by target customers.

The alternative to developing a minimum viable offering — developing a fully functional, full-scale offering without previously testing a simplified version — requires substantial investment during the early stages of the project, when market and technological uncertainty are at their highest levels. As a result, a company risks losing significant resources should some of its assumptions about the market and the technological feasibility of the offering prove to be incorrect.

Risk and Resources in Developing a Full-Scale Offering and a Minimum Viable Offering

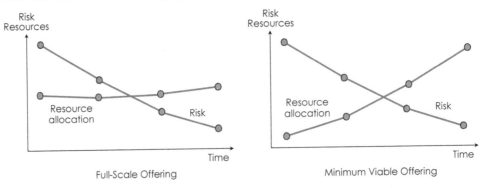

Full-Scale Offering   Minimum Viable Offering

The minimum-viable-offering approach aims to minimize the investment of resources during the early stages of the project when uncertainty and risk of failure are high and progressively increase investment in the offering as uncertainty and the corresponding risk of failure decrease. Rather than taking the risk of building a full-scale product or service, starting with a relatively simple version of the offering and validating this version prior to developing the final version reduces the uncertainty associated with bringing new products to market.

An important benefit of developing a minimum viable offering—in addition to its potential to minimize risk—is that it can offer a stream of revenue long before the launch of the final offering. Thus, the minimum viable offering can be thought of as the core module of the final offering that can be used to generate revenue. Such a revenue stream can offer a lifeline to startups running out of funds and provide greater independence to teams working in larger organizations.

Designing the minimum viable offering calls for weighing the key benefits sought by target customers against the resources necessary to create these benefits. In the ideal scenario, the key benefits sought by customers are those that require the fewest resources. This, however, is rarely the case. Most often, a company must prioritize benefits by weighing them against the resources needed to create these benefits. To this end, the development of the minimum viable offering aims to optimize its desirability (customer appeal), feasibility (achievability), and viability (company value).

Concept Validation

Concept validation assesses the soundness of the core concept underlying the proposed offering. Concept validation typically addresses two factors: the technological *feasibility* of the offering and its *desirability* in the eyes of target customers. Accordingly, to validate the concept, a manager should ask the following questions:

> *Is the offering feasible? Can a functional prototype of the offering be built? Can a fully functional version of the offering be built?*

> *Does the core concept of the offering appeal to its target customers? Does it address the identified customer need better than the alternative options? Are different attributes of the offering optimized to create customer value?*

Concept validation typically involves testing the key assumptions of the proposed concept in order to modify this concept—an approach referred to as *validated learning*. Validated learning begins with observing the market and identifying an unmet need, followed by formulating specific ideas (hypotheses), developing and testing a prototype capturing the core concept of the offering, and then testing this prototype. Unsatisfactory outcomes are followed by an analysis of the reasons for the failure, and the process is repeated until a satisfactory outcome is achieved.

The Validated-Learning Approach

Validated learning is based on data, not gut feeling. It typically involves empirical tests aimed at optimizing the initial concept by varying different attributes of the offering and evaluating their impact on its feasibility and desirability. For example, validated learning might involve identifying the optimal price point of an offering by varying its price and observing customers' reaction.

Stepwise product development, combined with experimentation aimed at verifying the key assumptions guiding the development process, is the hallmark of the validated-learning approach. Rather than conducting *all* market research prior to developing the offering—a legacy approach favored by many companies—validated learning is an iterative process of designing, testing, and modifying different aspects of the offering.

To proceed to the next stage in developing the business model, a company must validate the core concept underlying the company's offering. If the concept cannot be validated, the company must pivot and redefine the concept. If after multiple iterations the concept cannot be validated, the company must step back and reevaluate the underlying idea.

Market Research Tools in Concept Development

Concept development and validation are guided by *exploratory* studies that yield initial hypotheses (also used in the idea generation stage of business model development) and *experimental* studies that test these hypotheses.

Experimental studies aim to identify cause-and-effect relationships in the market. They achieve this goal by varying one or more aspects of the offering prototype and observing the effect of these changes on the offering's desirability. Unlike exploratory studies, in which an observer passively gathers information, experimental studies involve changing one factor (e.g., product design) in order to establish whether it has a causal impact on another factor (e.g., offering desirability). Because experiments are the main method used to establish causality, the terms *causal research* and *experimental research* are often used interchangeably.

Experimentation is important because it can help distinguish causality from spurious relationships. Causality involves relationships in which a change in one factor necessarily leads to a change in another factor. For example, for most products, lowering the price increases customer demand and sales volume. In contrast, a spurious relationship merely indicates that two or more factors follow the same pattern without asserting that this relationship is causal. For example, a company might observe that following the launch of a new advertising campaign the demand for its offerings increased dramatically. This, however, is insufficient to conclude that the new campaign caused the increase in customer demand, which might have been caused by a decrease in price that happened to coincide with the new advertising campaign. Therefore, the mere fact that one event precedes the other (e.g., the launch of an advertising campaign precedes the increase in customer demand) by itself is insufficient to claim causality. Only experimentation can prove causality by controlling for other variables that could influence the relationship between the factors of interest.

Because experiments involve at least two conditions—a control condition that is used as a basis of comparison, and an experimental condition that is used to measure the impact of the factor of interest—experimental research is often referred to as *A/B testing*.

BUSINESS MODEL DESIGN

Creativity is thinking up new things.
Innovation is doing new things.
—Theodore Levitt, author, *Marketing Myopia*

F ollowing the development of a viable concept is the design of a business model that delineates the ways in which an offering will create and capture market value. Unlike concept development, which focuses on the technological *feasibility* and the *desirability* of the offering, business model design also focuses on the offering's *viability* — the ability of the offering to create value for the company.

Designing the Business Model

Designing the business model involves identifying the *target market*, articulating the offering's *value proposition* in that market, and delineating the key attributes of the *market offering*.

- The **target market** identifies the market in which a company's offering aims to create value. Defining the target market involves identifying target customers, competitors, collaborators, the company, and the context in which these entities interact.

- The **value proposition** defines the value that the company aims to create and capture in the target market. Defining the value proposition involves identifying the value the company creates for target customers and collaborators as well as the value captured by the company.

- The **market offering** delineates the key attributes of the actual good that the company aims to introduce in the market. Defining the market offering involves delineating the product, service, brand, price, incentives, communication, and distribution aspects of the offering.

Business model design calls for developing a value map that identifies the market in which the company intends to compete and the ways in which the company's offering will create and capture value in the chosen market. This market value map, in turn, can include a series of specific value maps that delineate the way the company's offering creates value for its customers, collaborators, and stakeholders.

Designing the Business Model

Target market
- Customers
- Collaborators
- Company
- Competitors
- Context

Value proposition
- Customer Value
- Collaborator Value
- Company Value

Market offering
- Product
- Service
- Brand
- Price
- Incentives
- Communication
- Distribution

The key principles involved in developing the value proposition and the process of creating customer, company, and collaborator value maps were discussed in detail earlier in this book.

Business Model Validation

Business model validation assesses the ability of an offering to create market value. Because the success of an offering is determined by the degree to which it can create value for its target customers, collaborators, and the company, business model validation must address three sets of questions:

Does the offering create value for target customers? Does the offering fulfill customer needs better than the alternative options?

Does the offering create value for the company's collaborators? Does the offering enable the company's collaborators to achieve their goals better than the alternative options?

Does the offering create value for the company? Does the offering enable the company to achieve its goals better than the alternative options?

If the offering fails to create superior value for any one of the three market entities, the business model should be rejected and must be redefined. If after multiple iterations the model cannot be validated, the underlying concept must be redefined.

The Segway personal transporter illustrates the importance of validating the business model. Designed to be the ultimate transportation device in urban areas, the two-wheeled, self-balancing, battery-powered electric vehicle is controlled by the body movements of the rider rather than by a manual steering device. The Segway — its name is derived from the word segue, meaning smooth transition — was a technological marvel. Propelled by two electric motors and with multiple gyroscopic sensors controlled by a computer, the Segway could maintain near perfect balance while moving forward at a speed four times faster than that of a pedestrian.

The Segway was introduced amid great media buzz. Steve Jobs was quoted as saying that it was as big a deal as the PC, and John Doerr, the astute venture capitalist behind Amazon.com and Google, speculated that it was maybe bigger than the Internet, predicting that Segway might reach $1 billion in sales faster than any company in history. Segway's founder, Dean Kamen, projected sales of 10,000 transporters a week, which meant moving half a million units in its first year.

Neither of these forecasts materialized. Six years after its introduction, Segway had sold just 30,000 units, a far cry from the initial projections. After changing ownership several times, in 2015 Segway was acquired by one of its competitors, Chinese transportation robotics startup Ninebot.

What went wrong? The reasons for Segway's failure can be traced back to fundamental flaws in its business model.

The Segway functioned as advertised. Yet, it was unclear where one should use it. Riding on the sidewalk threatened many pedestrians and riding on the street posed danger to the rider. It was also unclear where one would park the Segway. Furthermore, even though it was dubbed a personal transportation device, at 100 pounds it was too heavy to carry and too big and cumbersome to put in a car trunk. The Segway was also awkward to use, sometimes causing people to fall (including former U.S. president George W. Bush, talk show hosts Ellen DeGeneres and Piers Morgan, and the owner of the Segway company, who lost control of his Segway and plunged off a cliff to his death).

Initially viewed as a cool novelty, the Segway quickly turned into an object ridiculed by many. People just didn't know what to make of it. Unlike a bike, it did not involve any activity on the part of the rider, and it was too slow compared to a car. The Segway was regarded as the laziest mode of transportation around — a sentiment that resonated with many consumers. Riding a Segway made some people feel geeky and made others uncomfortable at being the center of attention.

The Segway's price did not contribute to its popularity either. Priced at around $5,000 — the cost of a decent used car — the Segway was just too expensive for most consumers, who could not fathom why a device that seemed relatively simple would cost so much. The Segway was viewed as an overpriced toy that was out of reach for most of its target customers.

To sum it up, the Segway failed to create customer value on three key dimensions: It was challenging to ride in the city and was too heavy to carry (failing to create functional value); it was perceived to be dangerous and was ridiculed as a silly way to get around (failing to create psychological value); and it was too expensive for the average consumer (failing to create monetary value). The Segway was viewed as a nice-to-have toy, not a need-to-have transportation device. And even though it ended up being used in industrial and fleet applications by police, security guards, warehouse workers, and tour operators, the Segway never attained the mass adoption predicted by its creator.

Despite its revolutionary technology and a $100 million-plus investment in research and development, Segway ended up as a business fiasco. It was not the technology that failed Segway; it was its flawed business model that did not offer a viable value proposition for its customers. The Segway story shows, once again, that without a sound business model even the most ingenious innovation is destined to fail in the market.

Market Research Tools in Designing a Business Model

Business model validation can involve three types of market research: *exploratory*, *experimental* (both of which are also used in the idea generation and the concept development stages of business model development), and *descriptive*. Descriptive research builds on exploratory and experimental research to provide *quantifiable* information about the target market and the way in which the company's customers, collaborators, and competitors are likely to react to the company's offering.

Descriptive research is similar to the exploratory and experimental research used during the earlier stages of business model development. However, unlike exploratory and experimental research, which gathers qualitative information about the market and/or aims to establish a causal relationship between different market factors, descriptive research gathers *quantitative* information. Thus, descriptive research can provide information about the size of a given market, the demographic characteristics of the company's target customers, the market position of competitive offerings, and the sales volume attainable by the company.

Based on the way it is conducted, descriptive research can be primary or secondary. *Primary research* is original research conducted by the company to collect data to address a specific question of interest to the company. In contrast, *secondary research* involves searching and analyzing existing data that already have been collected by a different entity (a market research company, an academic institution, or a government organization). The key benefits of conducting primary research is that it is specific to the company's needs and provides current information that can help address a question that is of particular interest to the company. On the downside, conducting primary research tends to be relatively expensive and time consuming. Gathering secondary research, on the other hand, is relatively inexpensive and quick—benefits that can come at the cost of using data that might be outdated or not directly relevant to the specific questions the company aims to address.

An issue of particular importance when launching a truly novel (new-to-the-world) offering is estimating the size of the market and the speed with which customers are likely to adopt the product. In such cases, adoption can be estimated using *forecasting by analogy*—an approach that involves comparing the new offering to an established, functionally similar offering. For example, one could forecast the adoption of 4K televisions by examining the adoption of analogous products such as flat-screen, high-definition, and 3-D televisions. The key to forecasting by analogy is to identify an existing offering that is functionally similar to the new offering and likely to have the same market size and speed of adoption.

BUSINESS MODEL IMPLEMENTATION

*Thinking is easy, acting is difficult, and to put one's
thoughts into action is the most difficult thing in the world.*
—Johann Wolfgang von Goethe, German philosopher

Business model implementation is the process of turning the business model into a market reality. This process involves four main steps: *developing the resources* necessary for the business model to be put into action, *developing the offering*, *deploying the offering* in selected markets, and *expanding the availability of the offering* across the entire target market.

Resource Development

A company's market success depends on having the necessary resources to implement its business model. When designing the business model, a company typically has some but not all of the resources necessary for this model to succeed. Once the business model has been finalized, the logical next step is to develop—build, acquire, or outsource—the necessary resources.

Resource development can involve a variety of activities that aim to ensure the viability of the business model:

- Developing **business facilities**, including manufacturing (e.g., production equipment), service (e.g., call centers), and information technology infrastructure.

- Developing **supply channels** to ensure procurement of the ingredients from which the company creates its offering.

- Recruiting, training, and retaining **skilled employees** with relevant technological, operational, and business expertise.

- Developing the relevant **knowledge** (know-how) to implement different aspects of the company business model.

- Developing relevant **products**, **services**, and **brands** that can serve as a platform and create an ecosystem for the new offering.

- Developing **communication channels** that will inform target customers about the company's offering.

- Developing **distribution channels** that will deliver the offering to its customers.

- Providing **access to capital** to ensure availability of the financial resources necessary to carry out the implementation of the business model.

Most companies do not readily have all the resources needed to implement their business models. These companies can pursue two strategies: they can develop (acquire) these resources and/or they can obtain them by forging relationships with entities that have the required resources and are willing to collaborate to develop, procure, manufacture, distribute, and promote the offering.

Resource Development

Offering Development

Offering development involves turning the offering concept (prototype) into a market-ready offering. The development of an offering includes creating the actual product and service, building the brand, setting the retail and wholesale prices, defining sales promotions, and negotiating communication and distribution channels.

Offering development typically follows the development of resources needed to implement the company's business model. It involves deployment of the company's resources — its own as well as those of its collaborators — to develop, procure, manufacture, promote, and distribute the offering.

Developing the Market Offering

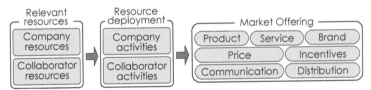

An important aspect of offering development is coordinating the deployment of company and collaborator resources and optimizing the timing of resource deployment to maximize their market impact. A key component of developing an offering is managing *resource velocity* — the speed with which resources need to be deployed to support the development and management of the company's offering. The more dynamic the market in which the company competes, the higher the resource velocity needed to succeed in this market.

Market Deployment

Market deployment involves informing target customers about the company's offering and making the offering available to these customers. Because large-scale rollouts are associated with greater uncertainty and higher costs, companies often first launch the offering in a few selected markets prior to introducing it to all target customers.

Selective market deployment aims to test the offering in a natural environment and observe how target customers, competitors, and company collaborators react to the offering. Because of its smaller scale, selective market deployment enables the company to be more agile in tweaking different aspects of the offering in order to maximize its market impact.

The subset of target customers that is the focus of the offering's initial deployment is also referred to as the *primary target*. The primary target is typically the low-hanging fruit that the company initially targets to prove the viability of its business model, fine-tune the offering, and generate a stream of revenue.

Identifying the Primary Target

| All potential customers (entire market) | Customers whose needs the company aims to fulfill (target customers) | Customers whose needs the company aims to fulfill first (primary target) |

The choice of the primary target is driven by three key factors: *target attractiveness*, *resource efficiency*, and *scale sufficiency*.

- **Target attractiveness** reflects the degree to which customers in a given market are likely to adopt the company's offering. Prioritizing customers based on their likelihood to adopt the offering typically follows *the path of least resistance*. Thus, the likelihood that customers will be among the first to adopt a company's offering depends on whether they (1) have the need that the offering aims to solve; (2) view this need as a pain point, a problem that needs solving; and (3) actively seek a way to address this problem. Customers for whom all three conditions hold are the most likely to adopt the company's offering and, hence, also the most likely to be chosen as the primary target. Customers for whom only the first condition holds—those who can benefit from the company's offering but are reasonably satisfied with the status quo—are the least likely to be selected as primary targets.

The Path of Least Resistance

☐ Customers with an unmet need (all target customers)

▨ Customers who recognize the unmet need as a problem that needs solving

▪ Customers who actively seek a solution to the problem

Path of least resistance

- **Resource efficiency** reflects the company resources required to communicate and deliver the offering to target customers. In choosing its primary target, companies often follow *the path of least resources*, determined by the company's ability to effectively and cost efficiently communicate and deliver the offering to these customers. For example, a company might choose its primary target based on the fact

77

that these customers are already aware of the company's brand and the company has the distribution channels in place to reach these customers.

The Path of Least Resources

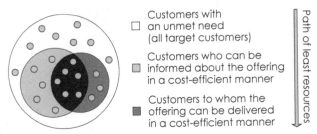

Customers with an unmet need (all target customers)

Customers who can be informed about the offering in a cost-efficient manner

Customers to whom the offering can be delivered in a cost-efficient manner

Path of least resources

- **Scale sufficiency** reflects the minimum size of the primary market needed to ensure that this market is viable from the company's standpoint. The choice of the primary market can be facilitated by the assessment of the *minimum viable target* — the smallest subset of target customers that is of sufficient size to generate the revenue needed to offset the company's costs of producing, promoting, and distributing the offering.

The primary target is defined by the overlap between the path of least resistance, the path of least resources, and the minimum viable scale. Therefore, when choosing a primary target to deploy a new offering, a company should focus on markets (1) in which customers have a burning unresolved problem that they are actively seeking to address (2) that can be easily reached by the company, and (3) that are large enough to enable the company to achieve its goals.

Market Expansion

Market expansion involves going beyond the primary target to include all customers for whom the company's offering aims to create value. Market expansion is the next logical step following successful deployment of the offering in its primary target market.

To expand beyond the primary target market, a company needs to (1) scale up the operations involved in the production of the offering, (2) promote the offering to all target customers, and (3) ensure that the offering is available across the entire target market. During market expansion, a company is typically moving upstream on the path of least resistance and the path of least resources, meaning that it aims to reach customers who are less likely to immediately recognize the value of its offering and who are more difficult to reach. As a result, the time, effort, and resources involved in market expansion are likely to exceed those involved in initial market deployment.

Because broader markets tend to involve customers with diverse needs and preferences, market expansion often involves a shift from a single offering to a product line comprising offerings tailored to the different needs and preferences of its customers. Thus, a company might start with a single offering targeting its most likely adopters and over time, as it expands to the broader market, introduce variations of this offering that are likely to appeal to different customers within its target market. The increased assortment of company offerings associated with market expansion, in turn, calls for additional resources to ensure the success of these offerings in the broader market.

3

THE BUSINESS MODEL TOOLBOX

IDENTIFYING TARGET CUSTOMERS

Where your talents and the needs of
the world cross, there lies your calling.
— Aristotle, Greek philosopher

Targeting aims to identify customers for whom the company will tailor its offerings. Targeting can involve individual customers, groups of customers making a joint decision, or market segments comprising multiple customers with similar needs. The key principle underlying the process of identifying target customers is *value creation*: The company should be able to create value for target customers who, in turn, should be able to create value for the company.

Strategic and Tactical Targeting

Identifying target customers has two components: *strategic* and *tactical*. Strategic targeting identifies which customers the company should serve based on the value it aims to create for and capture from these customers. Tactical targeting, on the other hand, identifies the ways in which the company can reach strategically viable customers in order to communicate and deliver the offering.

Strategic Targeting

Strategic targeting identifies the specific *customer need(s)* that the company aims to fulfill with its offering. For example, Uber aims to fulfill customers' need for convenient transportation, Groupon aims to fulfill customers' need to save money, Starbucks offers an assortment of high-quality coffee beverages tailored to customers' needs, and Warby Parker offers low-priced designer frames that appeal to customers' sense of fashion.

Strategic targeting involves trading off market size for a better fit of the offering's benefits with customers' needs. Instead of trying to reach the entire market with an offering that attempts to appeal to a wide variety of customers with diverse needs, strategic targeting calls for a conscious decision to ignore some potential customers in order to better serve others by tailoring the offering to their specific needs.

Deciding to deliberately forgo some potential customers is one of the most important and at the same time most difficult decisions a company must make. Many companies have failed because of their unwillingness to sacrifice market breadth and focus only on those customers for whom their offering can create superior value. The key to meaningful targeting is identifying not only customers that the company aims to serve but also those it will ignore. A viable business strategy is not possible without choosing to ignore some customers in order to better serve others.

Strategic Targeting: Identifying Customer Needs

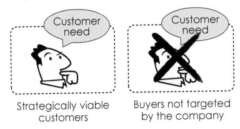

Strategically viable customers   Buyers not targeted by the company

Because strategic targeting reflects a company's ability to create and capture customer value, identifying strategically viable customers is the key to the success of an offering. Identifying target customers based on their needs, however, has an important drawback: Customer needs are not readily observable and therefore cannot be acted upon to communicate and deliver the company's offering. For example, it can be difficult to identify customers who might need convenient transportation at a given point in time (Uber), who are willing to expend effort to save money (Groupon), who might want a caffeinated beverage at a particular location (Starbucks), and who might be interested in designer eyeglasses (Warby Parker).

The challenge of identifying customers with a particular need is often referred to as *the identification problem*. The issue here is that without being able to identify ways to reach the strategically viable customers whose needs it aims to fulfill with its offering, the company would have to communicate the offering and make it available to *all* customers—an approach that in most cases is neither effective nor cost efficient. To address the identification problem, a company must link the unobservable customer needs to certain observable customer characteristics so that it can communicate and deliver its offering in an effective and cost-efficient manner. This process is referred to as tactical targeting.

The Identification Problem

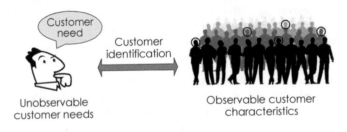

Unobservable customer needs   Customer identification   Observable customer characteristics

Tactical Targeting

Tactical targeting identifies effective and cost-efficient ways to communicate and deliver an offering to strategically viable customers by linking the need the company aims to fulfill to observable customer characteristics. These observable factors—referred to as the customer profile—involve four types of descriptors: *demographic, geographic, behavioral,* and *psychographic*.

- **Demographic factors** include customers' descriptive characteristics such as age, gender, income, occupation, level of education, religion, ethnicity, nationality, employment status, population density (urban or rural), social class, household size, and stage in the life cycle. For example, one of the commonly used demographic factors is that of generation, such as Baby Boomers (1946–1964); Generation X (1965–1981); Generation Y, also referred to as Millennials (1982–2000); and Generation Z (2001–present). When target customers are companies rather than individuals, they are identified by factors referred to as firmographics: size, organizational structure, industry, growth, revenues, and profitability.

- **Geographic (geolocation) factors** reflect customers' physical location. Unlike demographic data, which describe *who* the target customer is, geographic data describe *where* this customer is. Some of the geographic indicators—such as a customer's permanent residence, including country, state, city, and neighborhood where the customer lives—are more enduring, whereas others—such as a customer's current location at a particular point in time—are dynamic and frequently change over time. The proliferation of mobile devices that are uniquely tied to individual customers and have the ability to pinpoint their location has dramatically increased the importance of geographic factors in targeting.

- **Behavioral factors** reflect customers' actions. Common behavioral factors include customers' prior experience with the company's offering (e.g., customers new to the category, competitors' customers, current customers, or loyal customers), the frequency with which they purchase the offering, the quantity typically purchased, price sensitivity, sensitivity to the company's promotional activities, loyalty, mode of purchase (online or offline), frequently used retail outlets, role in the decision process (e.g., initiator, influencer, decider, buyer, or user), and the stage in their customer decision journey. Behavioral factors can also include the ways in which customers learn about new products, socialize, and spend their free time.

- **Psychographic factors** reflect facets of an individual's personality, including moral values, attitudes, interests, and lifestyles. Psychographics differ from demographic, geographic, and behavioral factors in that they link observable and unobservable characteristics of target customers. Although values, attitudes, interests, and lifestyles can be ascertained by directly asking individuals about them, psychographics are often not readily observable and instead are inferred from a customer's observable characteristics and actions. For example, a customer's interest in sports (psychographic factor) can be inferred from observing this customer's behaviors, such as subscriptions to sports magazines, viewing sports programming, gym membership, and purchases of sports equipment.

Because they are not readily observable, psychographics are similar to the customer need that the company aims to fulfill. However, unlike the specific customer needs the company aims to fulfill with its offering, psychographics are more general descriptors of an individual's attitudes that in most cases are not directly related to the company's offering. For example, a customer's affinity for sports does not necessarily mean that this customer needs a new tennis racket. Thus, psychographics can be viewed as a bridge between readily observable factors describing target customers (demographics, geolocation, and behavior) and the unobservable customer need that the company's offering aims to fulfill.

The proliferation of online communication and e-commerce has heightened the importance of psychographics by making customer moral values, attitudes, interests, and lifestyles readily accessible to companies. Using their customers' demographic, geographic, and behavioral data, social media companies such as Facebook, Google, and Twitter are able to construct actionable psychographic customer profiles. The same is true for traditional media companies, credit card providers, and online retailers that have data linking individuals' demographic, geographic, and behavioral profiles with their moral values, attitudes, interests, and lifestyle.

Tactical Targeting: Identifying the Customer Profile

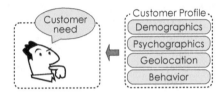

The Customer Persona

Targeting large groups of customers can make it difficult for managers to think of them as real people whose problems they must solve. Therefore, to facilitate targeting, companies often use fictional representations of their prototypical target customers, referred to as *customer personas*.

Personas make targeting more concrete by using a vivid representation of the typical target customer that managers can relate to. For example, consider a company developing smart thermostats that help customers save money on their energy bills. The company's target customers are all homeowners interested in lowering their energy bills. A customer persona, on the other hand, is a specific representative of the company's target customers. The customer persona might be an individual named Bob who is interested in saving money on his energy bills (the need that the company aims to fulfill). Bob is in his 40s, married, with a household income of approximately $80,000, has a college degree, lives in an urban area, and owns his own residence (demographic and geographic profile). Bob also prefers to shop online, is technologically savvy, has researched different energy-saving options, and is active on social media (behavioral profile).

The Customer Persona

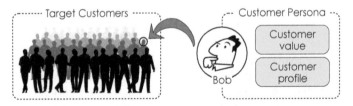

Clearly, the customer persona does not represent all target customers. Narrowing down the target segment to a representative individual, however, makes it easier to visualize the company's target customers and better understand how they are likely to respond to the company's offering. Because the customer persona is very specific, it might not adequately reflect the needs, demographics, geolocation, psychographics, and behaviors of all target customers. In such cases, a company might use multiple personas to account for the differences among its target customers.

Key Targeting Principles: Strategic Perspective

Strategic targeting is guided by the company's ability to develop an offering that will fulfill the needs of its customers better than the competition, and do so in a way that benefits the company. When evaluating the viability of a particular customer segment, a manager must address two key questions:

What value does the company create for its target customers?

What value do target customers create for the company?

Strategic Targeting: Key Principles

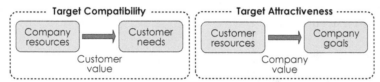

The answer to the first question is determined by the degree to which the company's resources are *compatible* with the needs of its target customers. The answer to the second question is determined by the degree to which target customers have the resources that make them *attractive* to the company. Thus, target compatibility and target attractiveness are the two key principles of strategic targeting.

Target Compatibility

The choice of target customers depends on the degree to which a company's resources are compatible with the needs of its target customers. Simply put, target compatibility is a company's ability to create customer value. Target compatibility is determined by the company's resources, including *business facilities, reliable suppliers, skilled employees, know-how, an established ecosystem, communication and distribution channels*, and *access to capital*.

- **Business facilities** include the manufacturing, service, and the information technology infrastructure necessary for creating the company's offering.

- **Reliable suppliers** are the entities that provide the ingredients for the company's offering.

- **Skilled employees** are the company's human resources with technological, operational, and business expertise.

- **Know-how** is the relevant expertise needed to run different aspects of the company business.

- **Established ecosystem** includes relevant products, services, and brands that can facilitate the adoption of the offering by its target customers.

- **Communication channels** are the processes and entities that inform target customers about the company's offering.

- **Distribution channels** are the processes and entities that deliver the company's offerings to its target customers.

- **Access to capital** involves access to the financing needed to design, produce, communicate, and deliver the offering to target customers.

In addition to being driven by the company resources, target compatibility also depends on how the company's resources compare to those of the competition. To create a sustainable value proposition, a company's resources must be superior to those of its competitors. Markets in which the company has unique resources to fulfill the needs of its target customers are the blue oceans in which it can create a sustainable business model. In contrast, markets in which the company and its competitors have comparable resources to fulfill customers' needs are the red oceans characterized by intense competition that makes developing a sustainable business model less likely to occur. The goal of strategic targeting is to identify customers whose needs the company has the resources to fulfill better than the competition and *make the competition irrelevant* by serving these customers in a way that competitors cannot.

Target Attractiveness

In addition to ensuring the compatibility of company resources with customer needs, effective targeting also depends on the attractiveness of the target customers, which reflects the degree to which customers have the resources — money, information, social influence, and time — to create value for the company. Factors that determine target attractiveness include *customer revenues, customer influence, customer loyalty,* and *customer costs.*

- **Customer revenues** reflect the money that customers are likely to generate for the company. Customer revenues are influenced by a number of factors, including the size of the customer segment and its growth rate, customers' buying power, and the quantity and frequency with which customers purchase the company offering.

- **Customer influence** reflects customers' ability to impact other potential buyers. Indeed, customers might be attractive not only because of the sales revenues they can generate for the company but also because of their social networks and ability to influence other buyers. For example, a company might target opinion leaders, trendsetters, and mavens because of their ability to promote and endorse the company's offering.

- **Customer loyalty** reflects customers' devotion to the company's offering and the likelihood that they will not switch to a competitor's offering. Because customer loyalty is important for ensuring the sustainability of the company's business model, targeting typically focuses on customers who are likely to create long-term value for the company rather than on customers motivated by short-term incentives and sales promotions.

- **Customer costs** reflect the expenses involved in acquiring and retaining target customers. These expenses include the communication costs of informing customers about the benefits of the offering, the costs of incentives that enhance the value of the offering, and the distribution costs of delivering the offering to target customers. The easier it is for the company to communicate the benefits of its offering and deliver this offering to a given customer segment, the more attractive the segment.

Key Targeting Principles: Tactical Perspective

Tactical targeting aims to identify ways to reach strategically viable customers by linking the unobservable customer needs the company aims to fulfill with the observable characteristics (profile) of these customers. The challenge that a company faces is reaching all strategically desirable customers without wasting resources on customers who are either unlikely to benefit from the company's offering or unlikely to create value for the company. Targeting that is too narrow is ineffective because it might overlook strategically important customers. Overly broad targeting, on the other hand, is not cost efficient because it wastes resources to reach customers that are unlikely to respond favorably to the company offering. Therefore, when evaluating different tactical targeting options, a manager needs to answer two key questions:

> *Does the company reach <u>all</u> of its target customers to communicate and deliver the offering?*
>
> *Does the company reach <u>only</u> its target customers to communicate and deliver the offering?*

The above two questions reflect the two main principles of tactical targeting: *effectiveness* (whether the company can reach all target customers) and *cost efficiency* (whether the company resources are deployed in a way that reaches only its target customers).

Targeting Effectiveness

The effectiveness principle means that the company's communication and distribution activities should reach *all* of its target customers. Effective targeting must ensure that all strategically viable customers — those whose needs can be fulfilled by the offering in a way that benefits the company — are aware of the company's offering and have access to it.

In the ideal scenario, often referred to as *sniper* targeting, the company communicates and makes its offering available to all strategically viable customers and only to those customers. This, however, rarely happens, especially in markets comprising a large number of individual customers. The two common errors that result in ineffective targeting involve choosing customer segments that are either narrow or off base. Narrow, or *slice-of-the-pie*, targeting reaches only a subset of target customers, thus missing the opportunity to capture a larger share of the market. Off-base, or *shot-in-the-dark*, targeting occurs when the company tries to communicate and deliver its offering to customers who are not strategically viable and are unlikely to respond favorably to the company's offering.

Tactical Targeting: Effectiveness

"Sniper" targeting (optimal)	"Slice-of-the-pie" targeting (too narrow)	"Shot-in-the-dark" targeting (off base)

○ Value-based segment
■ Profile-based segment

Targeting Cost Efficiency

The cost-efficiency principle means that the company's communication and distribution activities should reach *only* its target customers. The cost-efficiency principle is focused on managing resources in order to minimize (and ideally eliminate) expending resources on customers whose needs cannot be addressed by the company's offering or who cannot create value for the company.

The most common error that leads to inefficient targeting involves casting a communication and distribution net that is broader than the desired target customer segment. The problem with this approach, often referred to as *shotgun targeting*, is that it wastes company resources such as time, effort, and money by promoting and distributing offerings to customers who are not aligned with the company's strategic goals or are unlikely to purchase and use the company's offerings.

Tactical Targeting: Cost-Efficiency

- Value-based segment
- Profile-based segment

"Sniper" targeting (optimal)

"Shotgun" targeting (too broad)

Common Targeting Errors

Because identifying target customers is a central component of a company's strategy, poor targeting can have a profound impact on the company's business model. A systematic approach to identifying target customers can help the company sidestep some of the typical targeting errors. The three most common targeting errors include *focusing only on the customer profile, misidentifying customer value,* and *misidentifying the ways to reach target customers.*

- **Focusing only on the customer profile.** A common targeting mistake is focusing *only* on the observable characteristics of target customers—such as their demographics, including age, gender, and income—without considering the needs and the value sought by these customers. Focusing exclusively on the customer profile does not take into account the fact that customers with the same profile can vary in their needs and preferences; as a result, selecting customers based only on their profile might lead to targeting customers for whom the company cannot create value and/or who cannot create value for the company. To be meaningful, targeting should focus on both customer needs and customer profile.

- **Misidentifying customer value.** Another common targeting mistake is selecting customers that are either incompatible with the company's resources or cannot create value for the company. Selecting customers whose needs the company lacks the resources to fulfill precludes the company from creating value for these customers. Likewise, misidentifying the value that customers can bring to the company (because they lack buying power, because the customer segment is too small to meet company goals, or because target customers are too costly to serve) is problematic because the company is unable to capture value from these customers.

- **Misidentifying ways to reach target customers.** The third common targeting mistake is misidentifying ways to communicate and deliver the company's offering to its target customers. Incorrectly identifying the ways to reach strategically viable customers is problematic because it can lead to ineffective and cost-inefficient communication and distribution activities that waste company resources by reaching the wrong customers and ignoring the right ones.

Segmenting the Market

Many markets comprise thousands and often millions of customers, some of whom have similar needs that can be fulfilled by the same offering. In such cases, rather than developing individual offerings for each customer, a company might develop offerings for groups of customers—commonly referred to as *customer segments*—that share similar characteristics.

Defining Customer Segments

Segmentation groups individual customers by focusing on those differences that are relevant to the company's offering and ignoring those that are irrelevant. Grouping customers into segments enables a company to greatly reduce the variety of offerings it needs to develop for a given market, thus improving the cost efficiency of its offerings without sacrificing their effectiveness. In an ideal segmentation, customers within each segment behave with respect to the company's offering as if they were a single customer, yet across segments customers are likely to display significant differences in their response to the company's offering.

Market Segmentation and Targeting

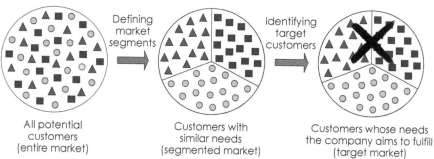

| All potential customers (entire market) | Customers with similar needs (segmented market) | Customers whose needs the company aims to fulfill (target market) |

Market segmentation and targeting can be illustrated as shown in the figure above, in which individual customers are represented by varying shapes and colors based on the differences in their underlying needs. For example, yellow circles might represent quality-focused customers, maroon triangles might represent price-sensitive customers, and blue squares might represent customers who are looking for a compromise between price and quality. In this context, the above figure depicts a scenario in which a company identifies three distinct customer segments and targets quality-oriented customers for whom it will develop high-end offerings, while ignoring the other two segments.

Like most business decisions, segmentation has its benefits and costs. The key benefit of segmentation lies in reducing the company's need to design, communicate, and deliver customized offerings to each individual customer and instead concentrate its efforts on a relatively small number of customer segments that group buyers with similar preferences. The key drawback is that grouping customers into segments can ignore potentially important differences that exist among individual customers.

When to Segment a Market

A key question in identifying target customers is whether to segment a given market and, if deciding to do so, how to segment it and how many segments to create. The answer to this question is closely linked to the concept of market heterogeneity.

A *heterogeneous market* is composed of customers who vary in their preferences and in the manner they tend to respond to a company's offering. Customers in a heterogeneous market are likely to seek different benefits, have different financial resources, and vary in the ways they can be reached by the company. Because customers in heterogeneous markets have different needs, they cannot be served by the same offering. In contrast, a *homogeneous market* is composed of customers with similar preferences who are likely to behave in a similar manner and, therefore, can be served by the same offering.

By identifying groups of customers with similar preferences, segmentation decreases market heterogeneity and creates homogeneous segments that are likely to respond in a similar fashion to the company's offering. Segmentation does not completely eliminate market heterogeneity; customers within individual segments still differ on a variety of factors. These residual differences, however, are less relevant to the company's offering and are unlikely to elicit different responses from customers with respect to the core benefits of the offering. To be effective, market segmentation should focus on the key factors that determine customer response to the offering and ignore factors that are not directly related to the company's offering.

The decision about how to segment the market and how many segments to create involves balancing the benefits of greater targeting accuracy and greater cost efficiency. Identifying a greater number of segments has the benefit of more accurately reflecting the needs of the customers within each segment, but on the downside, it tends to increase the cost of developing customized offerings for each segment and complicates the management of these offerings. Identifying fewer segments, on the other hand, has the benefit of being more cost efficient but has the downside of producing customer segments with diverse preferences, thus increasing the chance that the company's offering might not appeal to all customers in a given segment.

CREATING A COMPETITIVE ADVANTAGE

In football, everything is complicated
by the presence of the other team.
—Jean-Paul Sartre, French philosopher

To create a meaningful value proposition for its target customers, a company must design an offering that dominates the competition. Yet companies often launch products and services without a clear understanding of who their competitors are and why their target customers would choose their offering over competitive offerings. Unfortunately, these companies realize the importance of knowing the competition only after their offering is engulfed by it. Overlooking the competition prevents the company from delivering on one of the key principles of business model design: *The success of an offering is defined by its ability to create greater value for target customers than the competition.* Identifying the key competitors and creating a sustainable competitive advantage are the key components in developing a viable business model.

Identifying the Key Competitors

When managers are asked who their competitors are, it is not uncommon to hear the response: "Our product is unique. We don't have competitors." This is a very myopic and ultimately incorrect view. Virtually every offering has competitors. The reason why some managers think they have no competitors is because they are preoccupied with their own offering rather than with the customer need this offering aims to fulfill. Identifying the key competitors is vital to market success. Without knowing what other options are available, it is virtually impossible to design an offering that can create superior customer value.

To identify their competitors, managers should put themselves in the shoes of their customers and ask what need the company's offering aims to fulfill and what alternative means are available to fulfill this need. Thus, a company's competitors include not only the similar offerings that exist within the same industry but all means that can fulfill the same customer need as the company's offering. Customers typically do not care whether the means to fulfill a particular need exist within the same industry or come from different industries. What they do care about is whether an offering is the best way to address their needs.

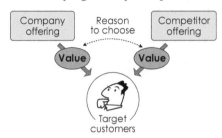

Identifying the Key Competitors

Depending on whether they belong to the same industry and/or product category, competitors can be either *direct* or *indirect*.

- **Direct competitors** are offerings that come from the same industry (product category) and aim to fulfill the same customer need as the company does. For example, Coca-Cola competes directly with Pepsi, Canon cameras compete with Nikon, and Marriott is competing with Hilton.

- **Indirect competitors (or substitutes)** compete across different industries (product categories) to fulfill the same customer need. For example, Coke competes with a variety of non-cola beverages, including juices and water. Canon competes with smartphones like Apple, Pixel, and Samsung. Marriott competes with peer-to-peer online apartment rental platforms such as Airbnb.

Because competition is defined relative to the customer need being fulfilled, not the industry or product category affiliation, both direct and indirect competitors present a viable threat to a company's business model. Therefore, to ensure market success, a company must look beyond the boundaries of the industry in which it operates and the product category in which it competes and design an offering that creates greater customer value than all alternative means of fulfilling the identified customer need.

A practical approach to identifying the key competitors is to evaluate the market through the eyes of target customers, examine the ways in which the company's offering fits into their lives, and pinpoint the alternative means that these customers can use to fulfill the identified need. In particular, there are three key questions that a manager can ask to identify the competition:

What are target customers currently doing to fulfill the need addressed by the company's offering?

If the company does not introduce its offering, what would these customers do?

What product, service, or behavior does the company's offering aim to replace?

What would target customers <u>not</u> choose if they were to choose the company's offering?

The first question aims to identify the competition by examining the *current behavior* of the target customers. Specifically, this question aims to uncover the default option (baseline) against which the company's offering will be evaluated. Identifying customers' current behavior is important because the value of an offering is defined relative to the option(s) that this offering aims to replace.

The second question seeks to identify the competition by examining the *counterfactual behavior* of target customers—their behavior in the absence of the company's offering. The option likely to be chosen if the company's offering were not available is the offering that will end up competing with the company's offering when it is introduced.

The third question aims to identify the competition by examining the *substitution behavior* of the target customers. Because customers often face resource constraints on factors such as time, money, and space, the introduction of a new offering would not necessarily result in an additional purchase; instead the new offering might replace an offering that customers have purchased in the past. Simply put, the introduction of a new offering does not mean that customers will end up buying *more* items but rather that they will buy *different* items. The item(s) customers might forgo buying in favor of purchasing the company's offering are this offering's competitors.

To illustrate, consider a company launching a new protein snack that offers a nutritious meal on the go for health-conscious consumers. To identify its competitors, a manager can start by examining the *current behavior* of its target customers—what snacks they currently consume. A manager can further examine the *counterfactual behavior* of its target customers and identify the means these customers can use to fulfill their need for on-the-go healthy snacks should the company not introduce its new snack. Finally, a manager can examine the *substitution behavior* that is likely to be displayed by target customers: How would their behavior change when the new snack is introduced? What would they take out of (or not put in) their shopping basket if they were to choose the new snack?

The above questions examining customers' current, counterfactual, and substitution behavior represent different ways to identify the competitive offerings. Because these three questions examine the same pattern of behavior of target customers, the answers to all three questions are likely to converge on the same set of competitors.

Assessing an Offering's Market Position

In an ideal world, a company's offering would dominate the competitive offering on all attributes. In reality, however, this is rarely the case. Because companies vary in resources, their offerings differ in the benefits they deliver to target customers. The relative advantages and disadvantages of an offering can be illustrated using a competitive value scorecard, which depicts customers' view of the performance of a company's offering relative to its competitors.

The competitive value scorecard identifies the key attributes that are important to target customers and highlights the advantages and disadvantages of the company's offering on these attributes relative to the competition. An offering's competitive advantage is defined by three factors: *points of dominance*, *points of parity*, and *points of compromise*.

- Competitive advantage (also referred to as points of dominance) involves the dimensions on which a company's offering is superior to the competition.

- Competitive parity (also referred to as points of parity) are the dimensions on which a company's offering is equal to the competition

- Competitive disadvantage (also referred to as points of compromise) are the dimensions on which a company's offering is inferior to the competition. These are the attributes on which customers must compromise in order to receive the unique benefits afforded by the offering.

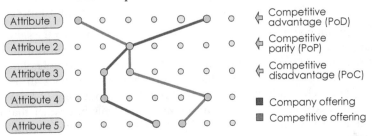

The Competitive Value Scorecard

The vertical dimension of the competitive scorecard delineates the attributes that create value for target customers, ordered in terms of their importance. The horizontal dimension reflects customers' valuation of the benefits derived from the company's and competitors' offerings on these attributes, with valuations increasing from left to right. Attributes on which the company's offering can create superior customer value relative to competitive offerings define its competitive advantage, attributes on which it is inferior define its competitive disadvantage, and attributes on which offerings are equivalent define the points of competitive parity.

Competition is not just about differentiation; it is about differentiation that creates greater customer value. Because competitive advantage is determined by an offering's ability to create superior customer value, only attributes that are relevant to customer needs can create a competitive advantage. Differentiating on attributes that are irrelevant and do not add value for customers does not lead to a competitive advantage. In fact, differentiation on irrelevant attributes might even decrease the perceived value of the offering if customers believe that the irrelevant attributes come at the expense of other more important benefits.

Competitive advantage is not merely about actual differences among competitive offerings; it is about differences that are noticeable and viewed as relevant by target customers. Minor differences in market offerings that are not noticed by customers or deemed to be irrelevant do not constitute a competitive advantage. For example, if customers cannot tell the difference in the performance of a 250- and a 260-horsepower car engine or if they find this difference meaningless, these offerings are at competitive parity. By the same logic, an offering might be viewed as having a competitive advantage even when its actual performance is identical to that of competitive offerings as long as this offering is perceived to be superior by customers. For example, two offerings might be at parity on their objective characteristics, but the stronger brand name associated with one of these offerings might make customers believe that this offering is, in fact, superior, giving it a competitive edge.

In addition to comparing customers' subjective evaluations of the offering's performance, the competitive value scorecard can also compare the offering's actual performance. The purpose of this analysis is to identify areas in which there is a discrepancy between an offering's objective performance and customers' subjective assessment of its performance. This is important because customers sometimes fail to discern actual differences that exist among offerings. Identifying such discrepancies is essential in order for the company to develop the appropriate strategy to improve customer evaluations of its offerings. Thus, if customers' belief that an offering is inferior stem from the fact that this offering actually underperforms the competition, the company should invest resources in improving the offering. In contrast, if the problem is customers' perception of the offering's performance rather than the actual performance of the offering, the company should focus its efforts on better communicating the benefits of its offering.

Creating a Sustainable Competitive Advantage

The competitive advantage of an offering reflects its ability to fulfill a particular customer need better than the alternative means of satisfying the same need. An offering's competitive advantage gives customers a reason to choose this offering instead of the other available options.

There are four core strategies to design an offering that dominates the competition: *differentiate on an important attribute, introduce a new attribute, build a strong brand*, and *create top-of-mind awareness*.

- **Differentiate on an important attribute.** This is the quintessential strategy for creating a competitive advantage. For example, Gillette sets itself apart from its competitors on the quality of the shave achieved with its products. Dollar Shave Club — an online shaving supplies retailer — has established price as its competitive advantage over premium brands such as Gillette. Online shoe retailer Zappos has differentiated itself from its competitors based on the level of customer service provided. BMW differentiates itself from the competition by the driving experience its vehicles deliver.

  Although differentiating on an important attribute is the most intuitive way to create a competitive advantage, it is often difficult to achieve because as the overall performance of all offerings in a category improves, they become more similar. For example, with the advancement of the overall quality of television sets, the differences among the available options have become less pronounced, making them more similar to one another in customers' eyes.

- **Introduce a new attribute.** Instead of enhancing an offering's performance on one of the existing attributes, a company might create a competitive advantage by introducing a new attribute that differentiates its offering. For example, Apple used design to differentiate its products from the competition. Dollar Shave Club introduced a subscription-based, direct-to-consumer shipping of shaving supplies. Warby Parker introduced a buy-a-pair/give-a-pair social responsibility program as an important dimension that differentiates it from traditional manufacturers of designer eyewear. Uber introduced a cash-free ride-payment to streamline the monetary transaction between customers and drivers. The Nest thermostat introduced machine learning as an alternative approach to controlling the temperature in one's home.

  The introduction of a new attribute is a powerful albeit rarely sustainable advantage. Indeed, when target customers value the new attribute, it is likely to be copied by competitors, which greatly diminishes the competitive advantage of the company pioneering this attribute. Therefore, to create a sustainable competitive advantage and stay ahead of the competition, a company must constantly seek new means of creating customer value.

- **Build a strong brand.** A powerful brand can be a source of sustainable competitive advantage and provide customers with a reason to choose the company's offering. As the old saying goes, nobody ever got fired for buying IBM. Even though IBM had many competitors with functionally similar offerings, the IBM brand signified reliability, making a big difference in customers' minds. Likewise, Harley-Davidson owes its success not only to the quality of its motorcycles but to a large degree to the strength of its brand in customers' minds. What separates Coca-Cola from the other cola drinks is not just its taste but its image, which has transcended national borders and cultural barriers to reach almost everyone on the planet.

  Although the brand can be viewed as an attribute of the company's offering, it plays a special role in creating a competitive advantage: It influences customers' perceptions of the offering on dimensions that are not readily visible, such as quality, reliability, and durability. In addition, brands like Harley-Davidson, Coca-Cola, and Warby Parker infuse the company's offering with a unique meaning that goes beyond the actual characteristics of the company's product and service, and creates value for its customers.

- **Create top-of-mind awareness.** When the available options are very similar in their actual performance, an offering can gain competitive advantage by becoming the first option that comes to a customer's mind as a means of fulfilling a given need. For example, Budweiser consistently promotes its flagship product so that when its customers think of a beer, the first brand that comes to mind is "Bud." In the same vein, GEICO spends tens of millions of dollars every year to ensure that when drivers are thinking about car insurance, they consider GEICO first. Likewise, McDonald's aims to be the first fast-food restaurant that comes to mind, ahead of its competitors Burger King, Wendy's, and Taco Bell.

  Having top-of-mind awareness creates a competitive advantage because the option that is considered first often becomes the default option against which the other options are evaluated. This is an important advantage since in the absence of a strong reason to choose an alternative option, buyers are likely to stay with the default option.

The above four strategies are the key ways in which a company can create and enhance its competitive advantage. Despite their common goal, these strategies vary in the ways they elicit competitive differentiation. The first two strategies — *differentiating on an important attribute* and *introducing a new attribute* — involve modifying the actual product or service that the company deploys in a given market. In contrast, the latter two strategies — *building a strong brand* and *creating top-of-mind awareness* — change the ways customers think about the company's products and services without necessarily changing the actual offering.

The four strategies are not mutually exclusive. They can be employed simultaneously to solidify an offering's competitive advantage. When deciding which strategies to pursue and how to prioritize them, a manager should choose the strategy that creates the greatest value for target customers, the company, and its collaborators. To create a meaningful advantage that makes the competition irrelevant, a manager must develop an offering that creates market value in a way that cannot be readily copied by the competition.

DEVELOPING A
POSITIONING STATEMENT

*Perfection is achieved, not when there is nothing left
to add, but when there is nothing left to take away.*

— Antoine de Saint-Exupéry, French
writer, author of *The Little Prince*

The positioning statement is an internal company document that outlines the key aspects of an offering's strategy. It aims to share the offering's strategy with the stakeholders involved in the development and management of the offering in order to coordinate their activities and align these activities with the company's business model.

The Positioning Statement as a Strategic Business Tool

The positioning statement is a succinct document — usually consisting of a single sentence — that delineates the key components of the offering's strategy. The primary purpose of the positioning statement is to guide tactical decisions related to the product, service, brand, price, incentives, communication, and distribution aspects of the offering. As such, the positioning statement seeks to communicate the essence of the offering's strategy to all stakeholders to ensure that their activities are aligned with the company's goals.

The positioning statement is important because different managers within the company might not have an accurate understanding of the offering's strategy: who the offering's target customers are, why they would choose this offering over a competitor's, and how this offering benefits the company. Accordingly, the positioning statement aims to provide a shared view of the offering's strategy to all relevant entities in the company.

In addition to ensuring that different company entities are on the same page with respect to the offering's strategy, the positioning statement aims to ensure that the company's collaborators — research and development and product design partners, advertising and public relations agencies, channel partners, and external sales force — as well as its senior management and investor stakeholders understand the company's business model. This is important because without knowing the offering's strategy the decisions and actions of the company's collaborators and stakeholders might not be aligned with the company goals.

The positioning statement is often confused with the brand motto and communication tagline. This is because all three capture certain aspects of the offering's strategy. Despite their similarities, however, they have different functions and are written for different audiences. The positioning statement is an internal company document aimed at company employees and collaborators; it is not intended to be seen by customers. In contrast, the brand motto and the communication tagline are explicitly written for the company's customers. Consequently, the brand motto and communication tagline use catchy, memorable phrases designed to capture customers' attention, whereas the positioning statement is written in a straightforward manner with a focus on the logic rather than on the form of expression.

For example, Gillette's positioning statement can be written as: *For all men who shave, Gillette provides the best shaving experience because it uses the most innovative shaving technology.* Gillette's brand motto is much more succinct and memorable: *Gillette. The Best a Man Can Get.* Finally, one of Gillette's communication taglines for its Fusion ProGlide razor highlights a particular aspect of its razor: *Less Tug and Pull.* Likewise, BMW's positioning statement can be articulated as: *BMW is the best vehicle for drivers who care about performance because it is designed to be the ultimate driving machine.* BMW's brand motto is: *The Ultimate Driving Machine.* A recent advertising tagline is: *BMW. We Make Only One Thing: The Ultimate Driving Machine.*[4]

Depending on the audience, there are three types of positioning statements: the *customer-focused positioning statement*, which articulates the offering's value proposition for target customers; the *collaborator-focused positioning statement*, which articulates the offering's value proposition for the company's collaborators; and the *company-focused positioning statement*, which articulates the offering's value proposition for the company stakeholders.

Customer-Focused Positioning Statement

The customer-focused positioning statement is the most commonly used positioning statement. A typical customer-focused positioning statement consists of several components: *the offering, its target customers, the frame of reference, competition,* and *the key benefit.*

- The **offering** is identified by its brand name or an alternative identifier (e.g., model number).

- **Target customers** are defined by their needs and/or their demographic/behavioral profile.

- The **frame of reference** is the product category with which customers associate the offering.

- **Competition** is the alternative options(s) that could fulfill the same need of the same target customers.

- The **key benefit** is the most important aspect of the offering that gives customers a reason to choose it. The key benefit could also involve justification of why the offering can claim this benefit.

Example: For [target customers] who seek [key benefit], [offering] is a better [frame of reference] than [competition] because [justification of the benefit].

```
For ..................... who seek ...............,
   (target customers)           (key benefit)

................ is a better ..........................
   (offering)              (frame of reference)

than ................... because ...................
      (competition)              (justification)
```

For the tradesman who uses power tools to make a living, DeWalt offers professional tools that are more dependable than any other brand because they are engineered to be tough and are backed by a guarantee of repair or replacement within 48 hours.

Example: [Offering] is the [frame of reference] that gives [target customers] more [key benefit] than [competition] because [justification of the benefit].

```
................... is the ..............................
   (offering)                (frame of reference)

that offers .................. more ...............
          (target customers)   (key benefit)

than ................. because ..................
      (competition)              (justification)
```

Mountain Dew is the soft drink that gives young, active consumers who have little time for sleep more energy than any other brand because it has a very high level of caffeine.

Example: [Offering] is a better [frame of reference] than [competition] for [target customers] because [key benefit].

```
.............. is a better ..........................
  (offering)               (frame of reference)

than ................... for ........................
      (competition)          (target customers)

because ...........................................
                   (key benefit)
```

Brita is a better source of drinking water than bottled water for price-conscious consumers because it costs less.

Example: [Offering] is a better [frame of reference] for [target customers] than [competition] because [key benefit].

```
.............. is a better ..........................
  (offering)               (frame of reference)

for ...................... than ....................
     (target customers)          (competition)

because ...........................................
                   (key benefit)
```

Gatorade is a better source of hydration for athletes because it rehydrates, replenishes, and refuels in ways that water can't.

Collaborator-Focused Positioning Statement

The collaborator-focused positioning statement is similar to the customer-focused positioning statement, with the main difference that it outlines the offering's strategy for company collaborators rather than for customers. The collaborator positioning statement follows a structure similar to the customer positioning statement and involves the same five key components: *the offering, the company collaborators, the frame of reference, competition, and the key benefit.*

Example: [Offering] [frame of reference] is a better choice for [collaborators] than [competition] because [key benefit].

> ....
> (offering)   (frame of reference)
>
> **is a better option for** ....
>   (collaborators)
>
> **than** .... **because** ....
>   (competition)   (justification)

DeWalt power tools are a better choice for retailers than Makita because they offer price protection from discount retailers.

Example: For [collaborators] who seek [key benefit], [offering] is a better [frame of reference] than [competition] because [justification of the benefit].

> **For** .... **who seek** ....,
>   (collaborators)   (key benefit)
>
> .... **is a better** ....
> (offering)   (frame of reference)
>
> **than** .... **because** ....
>   (competition)   (justification)

For mass-market retailers who seek to grow sales revenues and market share, Gillette Fusion offers a consumer staple that will generate higher profit margins than Gillette Mach3.

Company-Focused Positioning Statement

The company-focused positioning statement identifies the company stakeholders and outlines the offering's key value proposition for these stakeholders. The company positioning statement follows a structure similar to the customer and collaborator positioning statements and comprises the same five components: *the offering, the company, the frame of reference, alternative options,* and *the key benefit.*

Example: [Offering] is a better [frame of reference] for [company] than [alternative options] because [key benefit].

```
.............. is a better .............................
   (offering)              (frame of reference)

for ........................ than ......................
         (company)              (alternatives)

because ............................................
                    (key benefit)
```

DeWalt power tools are a better strategic option for Black & Decker than Black & Decker Professional power tools because they have a larger margin and generate greater sales volume.

Example: [Offering] is the [frame of reference] that gives [company] greater [key benefit] than [alternative options] because [key benefit].

```
.................. is the .............................
    (offering)              (frame of reference)

that offers .............. greater ...............
                (company)          (key benefit)

than ................... because ...................
       (competition)              (justification)
```

Fusion is the wet-shaving system that gives Gillette greater market share than Mach3 because it has higher profit margins.

DEFINING THE PROFIT FORMULA

Not everything that can be counted counts, and
not everything that counts can be counted.
— Albert Einstein, theoretical physicist

B ecause maximizing monetary value is the primary goal for for-profit companies, most of their offerings either directly or indirectly aim to generate profits. The way a company's offering creates monetary value for the company is reflected in its profit formula.

The Profit Formula

The profit formula articulates the ways in which a company generates monetary value for its stakeholders. On the most general level, a company's net income (profits) is defined by the difference in revenues and costs. Revenues, in turn, are a function of the unit price and the sales volume. Costs, on the other hand, involve *fixed costs*, which are expenses that do not fluctuate with the number of units produced (research and development, equipment, advertising, rent, and salaries) and *variable costs*, which are expenses that fluctuate in direct proportion to the number of units produced and sold (raw materials, incentives, and sales commissions).

The Profit Formula

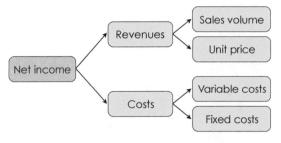

A company's profit formula is defined by the sales volume, unit price, variable costs, and fixed costs. Because some of the fixed costs (research and development and equipment) are amortized over a long period of time, they are prorated based on the proportion of the relevant resources used during the time frame in which the net income is being assessed. Thus, a company's profit formula can be summarized by the following equation:

Profit = Sales volume · Unit price – Variable costs – Prorated fixed costs

An important decision that a company must make is whether to maximize sales volume, maximize profit margins, or balance the two. Maximizing sales volume involves a *market-penetration* strategy in which the company achieves its profit goals by generating high sales volume, albeit at low prices (and, hence, low profit margins). Maximizing profit margins, on the other hand, involves a *market-skimming* strategy in which the company achieves its profit goals by charging high prices to generate high profit margins while sacrificing sales volume. In addition to market penetration and market skimming, there are a number of strategies that offer competitive prices and generate average sales volume without being at the extreme on either dimension.

Managing Profits by Increasing Sales Volume

There are two general strategies to grow sales volume: A company can either focus on its current customers by increasing the quantity and frequency of their purchases, or it can focus on acquiring customers that it does not currently serve. Although both strategies can increase sales volume, customer acquisition often plays a greater role in driving long-term profitability because of the inevitable attrition that erodes the company's current customer base. Growing sales volume through customer acquisition can, in turn, follow two paths: growing the size of the entire market by attracting customers who are new to the particular product category (market-growth strategy), and attracting customers who already buy similar offerings (steal-share strategy).

Managing Profits by Growing Sales Volume

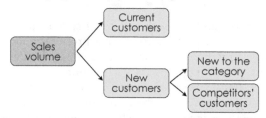

The *market-growth strategy* (also referred to as primary demand strategy) involves promoting the benefits of the entire product category without explicitly focusing on the differences between the company and competitors' offerings. Growing the entire market is particularly beneficial for companies that are most likely to gain from the influx of new customers to the market — typically companies with a dominant market share and those with a distinct benefit that is highly valued by target customers. The market-growth strategy also tends to be more effective in the early stages of a given category when sales growth is fueled by new customers entering the category, the competition is less intense, and the need to attract customers from competitors is less pronounced.

The *steal-share strategy*, on the other hand, involves promoting the benefits of the company's offering by comparing it with the competitive offerings. The steal-share strategy is often employed by smaller competitors aiming to gain share at the expense of their larger counterparts. Larger companies are generally less likely to benefit from comparing themselves to smaller competitors because such comparisons make customers aware of the smaller (and usually lesser known) competitors and might end up giving credibility to these competitors. The steal-share strategy is also common in mature categories where few new customers are entering the market and the competition for existing customers is relatively intense.

Managing Profits by Lowering Costs

Based on the type of expense, costs can be grouped into four categories: *cost of goods sold, research-and-development costs, marketing costs,* and *other costs* such as general and administrative expenses and the cost of capital. Different types of costs vary in their impact on a company's profit. Cost of goods sold typically is a variable cost, whereas research and development and many of the other costs tend to be fixed (meaning that they are not a direct function of the quantity produced and sold). Marketing costs fall into either the variable or fixed category depending on their type, with most advertising expenses being fixed costs and most incentives (discounts, rebates, and trade promotions) being variable costs.

Managing Profits by Lowering Costs

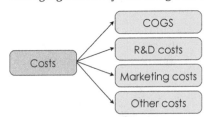

Marketing costs in general, and *customer acquisition costs* in particular, are a very important, yet often overlooked, aspect of a company's profit formula. Common acquisition costs include informing target customers about the company's offering, enabling them to experience the offering, providing promotional discounts, and offering a bounty for promoting the company's offering. Because acquisition costs are often viewed as marketing costs that will ultimately go away once the company gains its desired market position, these expenses are sometimes incorrectly excluded from the company's profit formula. Customer acquisition costs should be treated like any other cost. For a one-time-purchase customer, acquisition expenses can be considered as a variable cost; in cases where a customer's lifetime spans multiple purchases, acquisition costs can be considered fixed costs and are defrayed across the expected customer lifetime.

The J-Curve of Profitability

Because developing new offerings typically calls for an upfront investment, new product ventures are likely to have negative profits (losses) in the beginning. If the offering has a sound business model and is well managed, it will eventually recoup the initial losses and the net income will turn from negative to positive, forming a J-curve: accelerating losses in the beginning that start decelerating after reaching a turning point, followed by a break-even point at which the net income turns positive. The bottom of the J-curve is the point at which revenues equal expenses (excluding fixed costs) and cash flow turns from negative to positive. The point at which the profit line crosses zero is the point at which the offering starts generating profits (after covering the prorated fixed costs).

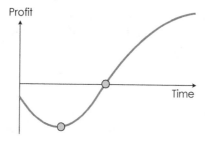

The J-Curve of an Offering's Cash Flow

An important component of the J-curve and the profit formula is the break-even point—the sales volume at which the revenues and expenses associated with an offering are equal, and beyond which profit occurs. The break-even volume is the ratio of fixed-cost investment to the unit margin (the difference between the sales revenue generated by a single unit of the offering and its variable costs). For example, an offering priced at $100 with variable costs of $50 and fixed costs of $50 million will require a sales volume of one million units [$50M/($100 – $50)] to break even and become profitable.

Break-even volume = Fixed-cost investment/(unit sales revenues – unit variable costs)

A key factor in determining the break-even volume is the unit margin, which is the profit the company makes on each unit sold, not counting fixed costs. In order to recoup the fixed costs—including the cost of research and development, equipment, and advertising—an offering should have positive unit margins. The greater the unit margins, the faster the company is able to recoup the fixed-cost investment and show a profit.

Value Monetization Strategies

Although all business models aim to create market value, they vary in the ways they monetize the company's business activities. Based on the source of revenues, there are three core value monetization strategies: *customer (direct) monetization, collaborator (indirect) monetization,* and *company (internal) monetization.*

- Customer (direct) monetization involves a scenario in which customers are the main source of the company revenues. For example, a manufacturer receives monetary payments from the customers who purchase its offerings.

- Collaborator (indirect) monetization involves a scenario in which the main source of revenue is the company's collaborators rather than its customers. For example, search engines, online content publishers, and app and game developers often receive payments from advertisers, who embed messages in their content, without being directly paid by end users. Instead of monetary payment, end users offer information about their needs, preferences, and behaviors, thus allowing advertisers to influence their preferences and gain mindshare.

- Company (internal) monetization involves a scenario in which other offerings in the company's own portfolio are the main source of revenue. For example, an offering might aim to promote another offering in the company's product line, as in the case of freemium and loss-leader offerings that enable the company to make money on the complementary offerings.

Quantifying the Profit Formula: Key Concepts

Income (profit-and-loss) statement: A financial document showing a company's income and expenses during a given period. It typically identifies revenues, costs, operating expenses, operating income, and earnings.

The Income (Profit-and-Loss) Statement

Gross Revenues	
Sales revenues	$ 18,000
Returns and allowances	(3,000)
Total (Gross) Revenues	15,000
Cost of Goods Sold	
Product costs	(4,500)
Services costs	(1,500)
Total Cost of Goods Sold	(6,000)
Gross Profit	9,000
Gross Margin	60%
Operating Expenses	
Sales and marketing	5,000
General and administrative	1,000
Research and development	1,500
Total Operating Expenses	7,500
Operating Income	1,500
Operating Margin	10%
Other Revenues (Expenses)	
Interest expense	(250)
Depreciation and amortization	(100)
Income tax expense	(400)
Total Other Revenues (Expenses)	(750)
Net Income (Earnings)	750
Net (Profit) Margin	5%

Gross margin is the ratio of gross (total) profit to gross (total) revenue.

$$\text{Gross margin} = \text{Gross profit}/\text{Gross revenue}$$

Gross profit is the difference between gross (total) revenue and total cost of goods sold. Gross profit can also be calculated on a per-unit basis as the difference between unit selling price and unit cost of goods sold. For example, if a company sells 100 units, each priced at $1 and each costing the company $.30 to manufacture, then the unit gross profit is $.70, the total gross profit is $70, and the unit and total gross margins are 70%.

$$\text{Gross profit}_{Total} = \text{Revenue}_{Total} - \text{Cost of goods sold}_{Total}$$

$$\text{Gross profit}_{Unit} = \text{Price}_{Unit} - \text{Cost of goods sold}_{Unit}$$

Gross revenue comprises the total receipts from a company's business activities.

Net income is the gross revenue minus all costs and expenses (cost of goods sold, operating expenses, depreciation, interest, and taxes) during a given period of time.

$$\text{Net income} = \text{Gross revenue} - \text{Total costs}$$

Net margin is the ratio of net income to gross revenue.

$$\text{Net margin} = \text{Net income}/\text{Gross revenue}$$

Operating expenses are the costs, other than cost of goods sold, allocated to generate revenue, including sales, marketing, research and development, and general and administrative expenses.

Operating income is the gross profit minus operating expenses. Operating income reflects the company's profitability from current operations without regard to the interest charges accruing from the company's capital structure.

$$\text{Operating income} = \text{Gross profit} - \text{Operating expenses}$$

Operating margin is the ratio of operating income to gross (total) revenue.

$$\text{Operating margin} = \text{Operating income}/\text{Gross revenue}$$

Contribution margin refers to the difference between revenues and variable costs and is typically calculated on a per-unit basis. Contribution margin can also be expressed as a percentage, calculated as the ratio of the difference between total revenue and total variable costs to total revenue (or the ratio of unit contribution to unit selling price). Unlike the gross margin, which includes some, but not all, variable costs (e.g., it excludes unit-based sales and promotional expenses), the contribution margin includes all variable costs

$$\text{Contribution margin (\$)} = \text{Revenue}_{\text{Unit}} - \text{Variable cost}_{\text{Unit}}$$

$$\text{Contribution margin (\%)} = (\text{Price}_{\text{Unit}} - \text{Variable cost}_{\text{Unit}})/\text{Price}_{\text{Unit}}$$

Marginal cost is the cost of producing one extra unit.

Trade margin is the difference between unit selling price and unit cost at each level of the distribution channel. Trade margins are typically calculated based on sales revenue (sales price) rather than based on cost (purchase price). A useful approach to analyzing trade margins is to map the channel structure and identify margins for each channel member.

Calculating Distribution Channel Margins

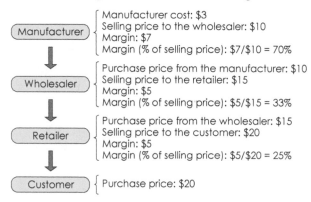

Compound annual growth rate (CAGR) is the year-to-year growth rate of an investment during a specified period.

Internal rate of return (IRR) is the annualized effective compounded return rate that can be earned on an investment (i.e., the yield on the investment).

Market share is an offering's share of the total sales of all offerings within the product category in which it competes. Market share is determined by dividing an offering's sales by the total category sales. Sales can be defined in terms of revenues or on a unit basis (e.g., number of items sold or number of customers served).

Market share = An offering's sales in a given market/Total sales in a given market

Return on Investment (ROI) is the net income as a percentage of the investment required for generating this income.

ROI = (Gain from an investment – Cost of investment)/Cost of investment

Return on sales (ROS) is the net income as a percentage of sales revenue.

ROS = Net income/Sales revenue

WRITING A BUSINESS PLAN

Plans are of little importance, but planning is essential.
—Winston Churchill, British politician

The business plan informs the relevant stakeholders about the company's business model and the process of making it a reality. The business plan presents a company's business activities in a logical and structured way to provide guidelines for managers and enable the company to implement its business model.

The Big Picture

The business plan is a written document that identifies the goal the company aims to achieve, outlines a specific course of action to achieve this goal, and provides guidelines for evaluating the company's progress toward this goal. It consists of five key components—*goal, strategy, tactics, implementation,* and *control*—which define the *G-STIC framework*.

- The **goal** identifies the ultimate criterion for success; it is the end result that the company aims to achieve. The goal has two components: the *focus*, which defines the metric(s) the company aims to achieve (e.g., net income), and the quantitative and temporal performance *benchmarks* to be accomplished.

- The **strategy** defines the company's *target market* and its *value proposition* in this market. The strategy is the backbone of a company's business model.

- **Tactics** define the key attributes of a company's offering: *product, service, brand, price, incentives, communication,* and *distribution*. These seven tactics are the tools that a company uses to create value in the chosen market.

- The **implementation** defines the process involved in creating the market offering. Implementation includes *developing resources, developing the offering,* and *market deployment*.

- The **control** evaluates the success of the company's activities over time. It involves two components: evaluating the company's *performance* and monitoring the changes in the market *environment* in which the company operates.

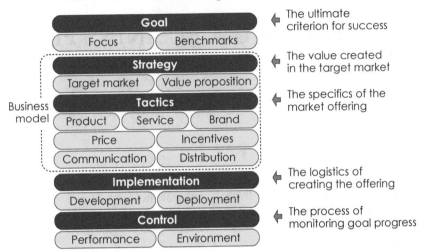

The G-STIC Action-Planning Framework

The Goal

The business plan starts with defining the goal that the company aims to achieve. This goal then becomes the beacon that guides all the company's activities. Without a well-defined goal, a company cannot design a meaningful course of action and evaluate its success. The importance of having a clear goal is captured in the words of the English mathematician and author of *Alice in Wonderland*, Lewis Carroll: *If you don't know where you're going, any road will get you there*. This insight applies to business as well: Wthout a set goal, a company is like a ship without a rudder.

Setting a goal involves two decisions: identifying the *focus* of the company's actions and defining the performance *benchmarks* to be achieved.

Defining the Goal Focus

The focus identifies the key criterion for a company's success; it is the metric defining the desired outcome of the company's activities. Based on their focus, goals can be monetary or strategic:

- **Monetary goals** involve monetary outcomes such as net income, profit margins, earnings per share, and return on investment.
- **Strategic goals** involve nonmonetary outcomes that are of strategic importance to the company such as growing sales volume, creating brand awareness, promoting other offerings, increasing social welfare, enhancing the corporate culture, and facilitating talent recruitment and retention.

Defining Performance Benchmarks

Performance benchmarks outline the quantitative and temporal criteria for reaching the goal.

- **Quantitative benchmarks** define the magnitude of the focal metric. For example, quantitative benchmarks can be formulated as "reach 10% market share," "increase retention rates by 12%," and "achieve annual sales of one million units."

- **Temporal benchmarks** identify the time frame for reaching the desired level of performance.

The goal focus, the quantitative benchmark, and the temporal benchmark answer three questions: *what* is to be achieved, *how much* should be achieved, and *by when* should it be achieved. To illustrate, a company might set the goal of generating net income (focus) of $10M (quantitative benchmark) in two years (temporal benchmark).

Strategy

The strategy delineates the value created by the company in a particular market. It is defined by the company's *target market* and its *value proposition* for this market.

- The **target market** delineates the market in which the company aims to create value. It is defined by five factors: *customers* whose needs the company aims to fulfill, *competitors* that aim to fulfill the same needs of the same target customers, *collaborators* that work with the company to fulfill the needs of these customers, the *company* managing the offering, and the *context* in which the company operates.

- The **value proposition** defines the value that the company aims to create in the target market. The value proposition has three components — *customer value, collaborator value,* and *company value* — which reflect the value created by the company for the corresponding market entities.

Tactics

Tactics define the actual *offering* that the company introduces in a given market. The tactics logically follow from the company's strategy and reflect the way the company will make this strategy a market reality. The tactics delineate the seven attributes that define the company's market offering: *product, service, brand, price, incentives, communication,* and *distribution*.

- The **product** is a good that aims to create value for its customers and entitle customers to the rights to the acquired good.

- The **service** is a good that aims to create value for its customers without entitling them to ownership of this good.

- The **brand** aims to identify the company's products and services, differentiate them from those of the competition, and create unique value beyond the product and service aspects of the offering.

- The **price** is the amount of money the company charges its customers and collaborators for the benefits provided by the offering.

- Incentives — volume discounts, price reductions, coupons, rebates, premiums, bonus offerings, contests, and rewards — are tools that enhance the value of the offering by reducing its costs and/or by increasing its benefits.

- Communication informs the relevant market entities — target customers, collaborators, and the company — about the specifics of the offering.

- Distribution involves the channel(s) used to deliver the offering to its target customers and the company's collaborators.

Implementation

Implementation defines the activities that aim to make the business model a reality. Implementation involves three key components: developing the company *resources*, developing the *offering*, and *market deployment*.

Resource Development

Resource development aims to secure the assets necessary to implement the company's business model. Resource development can involve creating *business facilities* that include manufacturing, service, and information technology assets; ensuring reliable suppliers; recruiting, training, and retaining *skilled employees*; developing relevant *products, services,* and *brands* that can serve as a platform for the new offering; acquiring the *know-how* needed to develop, produce, and manage the offering; developing *communication* and *distribution* channels to inform target customers about the company's offering and deliver this offering to them; and securing the *capital* necessary to develop these resources.

Offering Development

Offering development involves the processes that transform the company's business model into an actual good that is communicated and delivered to the company's target customers. Offering development involves managing the flow of information, materials, labor, and money in order to create the offering that the company will deploy in its target market. In addition, offering development involves designing the *product* (procurement, inbound logistics, and production) and *service* (installation, support, and repair activities); building the *brand*; setting retail and wholesale *prices* and *incentives* (coupons, rebates, and price discounts); designing the means of *communication* (message, media, and creative solution); and setting the *distribution* (warehousing, order fulfillment, and transportation).

Market Deployment

Market deployment logically follows the process of developing an offering by delineating the process of bringing the offering to the market. Market deployment involves setting the timing of the offering's market launch, defining the resources involved in this launch, and determining the scale of the launch.

Market deployment can be selective, initially focusing on specific markets in order to assess the market reaction to the offering, or it can involve a large-scale rollout across all target markets. In cases of selective market deployment, the business plan defines the primary market in which the offering will first be introduced and outlines the key activities associated with the launch of the offering. The business plan further identifies the timing and the processes involved in expanding the offering beyond the primary market so that it can reach all target customers and achieve its full market potential.

Control

Business models are not static; once developed they evolve over time. The constantly changing business environment requires companies to be agile and continuously realign their business models—a process outlined in the control section of the business plan. The primary function of controls is to inform the company whether to proceed with its current course of action, whether to reevaluate its actions and realign the underlying business model, or whether to abandon its current course of action and pivot its business model to better reflect the current market realities. Controls involve two key components: evaluating the company's performance and monitoring the market environment.

Performance Evaluation

Evaluating performance involves tracking the company's progress toward its goal, defined by its focus and benchmarks. Performance evaluation can lead to one of two outcomes: either a company is making adequate goal progress, or there is a discrepancy (performance gap) between the desired and the actual performance. When the progress is adequate, the company can stay the course with its current action plan. In contrast, when performance evaluation reveals a gap, the company's action plan must be modified to put the company back on track toward achieving its goal.

Monitoring the Environment

Monitoring the environment aims to identify market opportunities and threats. It enables the company to take advantage of new opportunities such as favorable government regulations, a decrease in competition, or an increase in consumer demand, as well as to counteract potential threats such as unfavorable government regulations, an increase in competition, or a decline in customer demand. Monitoring the environment in which the company operates is one of the prerequisites of business agility and a necessary condition for sustainability of the company's business model.

The Business Plan as a Written Document

A company's business plan is captured in a written document that aims to communicate the proposed course of action to relevant stakeholders: company employees, collaborators, and investors. The business plan comprises four main components: *an executive summary, a situation overview, an action plan,* and *exhibits*.

- The **executive summary** is the elevator pitch for the business plan; it is a streamlined and succinct overview of the company's goal and the proposed course of action.

- The **situation overview** outlines the key aspects of the market in which the company operates.

- The action plan, defined by the G-STIC framework, is the core of the business plan. It identifies the *goal* the company aims to achieve, the offering's *strategy* (the target market and value proposition), the offering's *tactics* (product, service, brand, price, incentives, communication, and distribution), the *implementation* process (developing the resources, developing the offering, and market deployment) that makes the offering's business model a market reality, and *control* procedures needed to assess the company's performance and monitor for changes in the environment in which it operates.

- Exhibits help streamline the business plan by separating the less important and more technical aspects of the plan into a distinct section in the form of tables, charts, and appendices.

The ultimate goal of the business plan is to guide a company's actions. Accordingly, the backbone of the business plan is the G-STIC framework that delineates the company's goal and the proposed course of action. The other components of the business plan—the executive summary, situation analysis, and exhibits—aim to facilitate an understanding of the logic underlying the plan and provide specifics for the proposed course of action.

4

BUSINESS MODEL EXAMPLES

HOW TO BECOME A UNICORN:
FIVE BILLION-DOLLAR STARTUPS

*The problems that exist in the world today cannot be
solved by the level of thinking that created them.*
— Albert Einstein, theoretical physicist

For most people, a *unicorn* (literally meaning "one-horn") is a mythical creature with a large, pointed, spiraling horn projecting from its forehead. For startups and venture investors, however, a *unicorn* means something entirely different; it refers to a startup valued at over $1 billion. Not every company that has become a unicorn has been able to sustain its early success. Yet, startups that have reached $1 billion status merit attention, and their business models can help illustrate the key aspects of the process of creating market value.

This section outlines the business models of five startups: *Dollar Shave Club*, a subscription-based retailer of low-priced razors and blades; *Warby Parker*, a trendy fashion alternative to high-priced designer prescription eyeglasses; *Nest Labs*, the creator of a thermostat that automates home temperature management; *Uber*, an alternative to taxi and limo services, and *Zenefits*, a comprehensive human resource solution for small businesses.[5]

These five companies share a number of commonalities. All five aimed to disrupt the ways in which their industries operate. All five had to design new business models and convince their customers, collaborators, and stakeholders of the viability of their market offering. And all five became unicorns, reaching a valuation of $1 billion or higher within five years of their launch.

Despite their common aspects, these companies vary on a number of dimensions. The most obvious difference is the diverse industries in which they operate. Dollar Shave Club distributes shaving products, Warby Parker sells fashion eyeglasses, Nest Labs makes home temperature automation devices, Uber connects drivers with those needing a ride, and Zenefits helps small businesses manage employee benefits.

The companies also vary in the roles they play in the market. Dollar Shave Club is a retailer that distributes products developed and produced by a third party, Warby Parker designs and distributes its own products, Nest Labs designs products that are distributed through a variety of retailers, Uber is an online platform that connects riders with drivers, and Zenefits is a business-to-business service provider. Dollar Shave Club offers its products as a subscription service, Warby Parker sells products that do not require ongoing service, Nest Labs distributes an intricate combination of products and services, Uber offers services that transport people and physical objects, and Zenefits offers a cloud-based service solution.

The business models of these companies also vary in the type of customer value they create. The primary benefit created by Dollar Shave Club is monetary (low price), with functionality (convenience) as a secondary benefit. The primary benefit of Warby Parker is psychological (self-expression), with the monetary aspect (low price) as a secondary benefit. The primary benefit of Nest is functionality (ease of operation), with the monetary aspect (low energy bill) as a secondary benefit. Uber's primary benefit is functional (fast and convenient transportation), with the psychological aspect (having a "personal driver") and monetary aspect (low price) as secondary benefits. The primary benefit of Zenefits is functionality (streamlining employee benefit management), with the monetary aspect (free) as a secondary benefit.

The value maps underlying the business models of these five companies vary in complexity. The Dollar Shave Club and Zenefits value maps outlined in this book are relatively simple and focus only on the value created for customers and the company, without discussing collaborators in detail. The value maps for Warby Parker and Uber are more complex and depict the value their offerings create for target customers, the company, and collaborators. Finally, Nest's value map outlines the value created for target customers and the company, as well as for several of its collaborators.

Despite their early success, the five companies are not presented here to epitomize a winning business model. The primary goal of these examples is to illustrate the key aspects of developing a business model rather than to endorse the business models of the discussed companies. Each of these companies faces distinct challenges that must be overcome to solidify its market position. As market conditions change, all five companies might not be able to sustain their growth trajectory: some could succeed and others could end up engulfed by emerging competitors.

Dollar Shave Club: Disrupting the Grooming Industry

Dollar Shave Club is a subscription-based online retailer of low-priced razors and blades. From a strategic standpoint, Dollar Shave Club's business model is B2C (business-to-consumer), with consumers generating company revenues. From a tactical standpoint, Dollar Shave Club employs a *subscription model* (a monthly subscription rather than purchase of individual items); a *razor-and-blades model* (the razor handle is given away, with profits generated by the sales of cartridges); and a *direct-to-consumer distribution model* (without relying on third-party retailers). The Dollar Shave Club market value map presents a relatively simple scenario depicting the value relations between the company and its customers. Even though Dollar Shave Club collaborates with entities that supply the products it sells, the core of the business model is the value exchange between the company and its customers.

Warby Parker: Building a Lifestyle Brand

Warby Parker is a direct-to-consumer provider of competitively priced, trendy prescription eyeglasses. From a strategic standpoint, the Warby Parker business model is B2C, with customers generating the company's revenues. From a tactical standpoint, Warby Parker involves a *direct-to-consumer model* (direct distribution with minimal reliance on third-party retailers), a *free-trial model* (customers can order and try on up to five pairs of frames at a time), and a *one-for-one model* (for each pair purchased, Warby Parker donates money to distribute a pair of glasses to someone in need). Warby Parker's market value map depicts all three aspects of the value creation process, illustrating the ways in which the company creates value not only for its customers and stakeholders but also for its collaborators—boutique retailers renting space to Warby Parker to serve as its showrooms.

Nest Labs: Designing the Connected Home

Nest Labs is the creator of the *Nest* thermostat that automates home temperature management. From a strategic standpoint, Nest's business model is B2C, with customers generating the company's revenues. From a tactical standpoint, Nest involves a *market-skimming model* (product pricing is at a premium to the majority of the competitors), an *omnichannel model* (using brick-and-mortar and online distribution channels), a *push model* (offering promotional incentives to channel partners to push its products to consumers), and a *pull model* (offering promotional incentives directly to customers in order to create demand for its products). Nest's value map illustrates a relatively complex scenario that involves several collaborators fulfilling different market functions. Accordingly, the Nest business model includes several collaborator value maps that delineate the ways the offering creates value for Nest partners: retailers, contractors, and developers.

Uber: Creating the Perfect Ride

An alternative to taxi and limo services, Uber is a ridesharing platform connecting drivers with those needing a ride. From a strategic standpoint, Uber's business model is C2C (customer-to-customer), with customers generating the company's revenues. From a tactical standpoint, Uber involves a *rent model* (ride-sharing is a service that aims to replace car ownership), a *market-penetration model* (services are priced at a discount to the majority of the market options in order to gain rapid adoption), a *surge-pricing model* (premium pricing aims to align demand with supply), and a *direct-to-consumer model* (the service is offered directly to consumers without relying on a third party). Uber's value map illustrates a large-scale global network that connects hundreds of thousands of collaborators (drivers) with millions of customers in a scenario where collaborators are individuals rather than business entities.

Zenefits: Managing Employee Benefits for the Small Business

Zenefits offers comprehensive human resource management solutions for small businesses. From a strategic standpoint, Zenefits' business model is B2B (business-to-business), with collaborators (benefit providers) rather than customers (small businesses) generating the company's revenues. From a tactical standpoint, Zenefits involves a *software-as-a-service (SaaS) model* (the offering is a service rather than a software package), a *subscription model* (services are offered on a recurring basis), and a *direct-to-customer model* (the service is offered directly to consumers without relying on a third party). Unlike the first four examples, which depict companies operating in business-to-consumer markets, the Zenefits value map involves a business-to-business market. The Zenefits example shows that the market value maps have the same structure and follow the same logic for both consumer and business markets.

DOLLAR SHAVE CLUB:
DISRUPTING THE GROOMING INDUSTRY

Anyone can build market share and, if you set your
prices low enough, you can get the whole market.
— David Packard, co-founder of Hewlett-Packard

Dollar Shave Club is an online retailer selling razors and cartridges on a subscription basis, with prices starting as low as $1 per month. Founded by Mark Levine and Michael Dubin in July 2011, Dollar Shave Club acquired awareness in early 2012 after Dubin's YouTube video went viral, gaining nearly five million views in the first three months and attracting the attention of the mass media.[6]

Building on its initial success, Dollar Shave Club expanded beyond razors and cartridges, offering its own line of grooming products, including shaving cream and after-shave lotion. Unlike its razors and cartridges, which on a per-unit basis were priced lower than the leading brand, Dollar Shave Club's grooming products were priced at a premium to similar products in the market.

Three years into its launch, Dollar Shave Club had raised over $160 million in venture capital funding from a group of investors that included Kleiner Perkins Caufield & Byers, Andreessen Horowitz, Shasta Ventures, White Star Capital, and Felicis Ventures. By 2015 it had amassed over three million customers, capturing about 8% of the $3 billion U.S. market for razors and cartridges, and generating over $150 million in revenue. In 2016, only four years after its launch, Dollar Shave Club became the second-largest men's razor seller in the United States, topped only by Gillette. In the summer of 2016, Unilever acquired Dollar Shave Club for $1 billion in an all-cash deal.

Dollar Shave Club Market Value Map

Dollar Shave Club's market value map delineates the target market, the company's offering in this market, and the ways in which this offering creates value for its target customers, its collaborators, and the company stakeholders.

Dollar Shave Club Market Value Map

Target Market	
Customers	All men who shave and are looking to save money on razors and cartridges
Collaborators	Dorco—Korean manufacturer that supplies razors and cartridges to Dollar Shave Club
Company	Dollar Shave Club—an online distributor of namesake-branded shaving systems and supplies
Competitors	Shaving systems (razors and cartridges) manufactured by Gillette, Schick, and others
Context	Rapid growth of online retailing, widespread dissatisfaction with the high prices of Gillette cartridges

Value Proposition	
Customer Value	Monetary savings and shopping convenience
Collaborator Value	Incremental revenues
Company Value	Generate profits, gain market position, build a strong brand, and create a loyal customer base

Market Offering	
Product	Shaving system (razor and cartridges) and grooming products. Three-tier offering that includes 2-, 4-, and 6-bladed cartridge options
Service	Monthly shipping of the selected items
Brand	Brand name: Dollar Shave Club; Brand associations: savings and convenience; Brand motto: "Shave Money. Shave Time"
Price	$1/month + $2 shipping/handling (2-bladed cartridge) $6/month (4-bladed cartridge) $9/month (6-bladed cartridge)
Incentives	Free handle included with the first order; free first month of The Executive razor shipments with the purchase of shave butter for $8
Communication	YouTube.com, banner advertising, keyword search, targeted emails, DollarShaveClub.com,
Distribution	DollarShaveClub.com for placing orders; UPS and the U.S. postal service for order delivery

Target Market

- **Customers:** All price-conscious men who shave.

- **Collaborators:** Dorco—Korean manufacturer that supplies razors and cartridges to Dollar Shave Club.

- Company: Dollar Shave Club is an online distributor of namesake-branded shaving systems and shaving supplies. Its core competency is in brand building and direct-to-consumer communication and distribution.

- Competition: Shaving systems (razors and cartridges) manufactured by other companies, primarily Gillette.

- Context: Rapid growth of online retailing, increased dissatisfaction with high price of shaving cartridges, especially those of the market leader, Gillette.

Value Proposition

- **Customer value proposition:** Monetary savings and shopping convenience.

- **Collaborator value proposition:** Incremental revenues.

- **Company value proposition:** Generate profits, gain market position, build a strong consumer brand, and create a loyal customer base.

Market Offering

- **Product:** Shaving system (razor handle and cartridges) and various grooming products (shaving cream, post-shave cream, and hair pomade). Three-tier (good-better-best) offering with 2-bladed, 4-bladed, and 6-bladed cartridge options.

- **Service:** Monthly shipping of the selected items.

- **Brand:** Dollar Shave Club. *Brand logo:* Circle with two crossed razors in the middle and letters D, S, and C surrounding the razors. *Brand motto:* Shave Money. Shave Time. *Sub-brands:* The Humble Twin (2-bladed cartridge), The 4X (4-bladed cartridge), The Executive (6-bladed cartridge), Dr. Carver's (grooming products). *Key brand associations:* Savings and convenience.

- **Price:** $1/month + $2 shipping/handling (2-bladed cartridge); $6/month (4-bladed cartridge); $9/month (6-bladed cartridge).

- **Incentives:** Free handle included with the first order; free first month of The Executive razor blades with a qualified purchase.

- **Communication:** YouTube.com, advertising on third-party websites, keyword search, targeted emails, social media, company website (DollarShaveClub.com).

- **Distribution:** DollarShaveClub.com website for order placement; UPS and the U.S. postal service for order delivery.

Dollar Shave Club Customer Value Map

Target Customers

- **Customer needs:** Save money on shaving.

- **Customer profile:** All men who shave.

Competition

- **Key competitors:** Gillette razors and cartridges, which account for more than 60% of the U.S. retail shaving market and 20% of the online shaving market.

- **Competitor value proposition:** Superior shaving experience reflected in Gillette's motto: *Gillette. The Best a Man Can Get.*

- **Attributes of the competitive offerings:** Gillette Mach 3 (3-bladed cartridge) is sold in 2-, 5-, 10-, and 15-packs, and is priced at $2–$3 (MSRP) per cartridge, with larger packs offering a lower per-cartridge price. Gillette Fusion (5-bladed cartridge) is sold in 4-, 8-, 12-, and 16-packs, and is priced at $4.50–$6 (MSRP) per cartridge, with larger packs offering a lower per-cartridge price. Gillette offers significant promotional discounts to retailers, resulting in consumer prices that are 20%–50% lower than the suggested retail prices.

Customer Value Proposition

- **Customer value equation**

  - *Benefits:* Clean shave, convenient delivery of replacement cartridges (functional benefit); satisfaction from saving money and from having a viable alternative to the leading brand (psychological benefit); monetary savings relative to the market leader (monetary benefit).

  - *Costs:* Risk that the product might not work as intended (functional cost), time/effort involved in signing up for the service, potential regret if the new product does not deliver on its promise (psychological cost), price paid for the subscription (monetary cost).

- **Competitive advantage**

  - *Points of dominance:* Monetary savings and convenience.
  - *Points of parity:* Product quality and shaving experience.

- **Reason to choose:** Same performance as Gillette at a lower price.

Dollar Shave Club Customer Offering

Offering	Features	Customer value
Product	2-bladed, 4-bladed, and 6-bladed cartridges with lubricating strip, and a trimmer edge on the back (6-bladed cartridges)	Offer smooth shave and facilitate trimming
	Grooming products (shave butter, post-shave cream)	Improve the shaving experience
Service	Subscription service	Offers convenience
	Online customer support	Addresses customer issues
Brand	*Brand name:* Dollar Shave Club	Conveys the notion of savings based on a subscription
	Logo: Circle with two crossed razors in the middle and letters D, S, and C surrounding the razors	Creates a visual image of the brand and conveys the nature of the offering (razors)
	Motto: Shave Money. Shave Time.	Communicates the core benefits: savings and convenience
	Sub-brands: The Humble Twin (2-bladed cartridge), The 4X (4-bladed cartridge), The Executive (6-bladed cartridge), Dr. Carver's (grooming products)	Help customers differentiate between the different types of razors; personified sub-brands facilitate a personal connection with customers
	Key brand associations: Savings and convenience	Facilitates the creation of a relevant brand image

Price	$1/month + $2 shipping and handling (2-bladed cartridge) $6/month (4-bladed cartridge) $9/month (6-bladed cartridge)	Per-cartridge cost to the consumer is lower than Gillette
	$8 (shave butter), $9 (post-shave cream)	Cost to the consumer is higher than Gillette's
	No tax outside of California	Additional monetary savings
Incentives	Free first month of The Executive razor blades with purchase of shave butter	Offers enticement to try Dollar Shave Club's high-end razor
	Free razor handle	Reduces the upfront cost of trying the Dollar Shave Club
Communication	*Message:* Dollar Shave Club is a cheaper and convenient alternative to big brands (Gillette)	Communicates the key benefits of the Dollar Shave Club: savings and convenience
	Media: YouTube.com, DollarShaveClub.com, advertising on third-party websites, keyword search, targeted emails, social media	Broad range of media informs target customers about the benefits of Dollar Shave Club
	Creative format: Simple, witty language; "Shave Money. Shave Time," "A great shave for a few bucks a month. No commitment. No fees."	Visually pleasing, easy-to-understand messages explain Dollar Shave Club benefits
Distribution	DollarShaveClub.com website for order placement UPS and the U.S. postal service for order delivery	Easy ordering; products are delivered directly to customer's home

Dollar Shave Club Company Value Map

The Company

- Company profile: Dollar Shave Club is an online distributor of namesake-branded shaving systems and shaving supplies. The company's core competency is in brand building and direct-to-consumer distribution.
- Company goals: Generate revenues and profits (monetary goal); gain market position, build a strong brand, and create a loyal customer base (strategic goal).

Alternative Options

- Key alternatives: Investing in a faster growing industry. Within the shaving industry, alternative options include partnering with brick-and-mortar retail channels and investing in the development and production of razors and cartridges.

- Value proposition of the alternative options: Investing in a faster growing industry has the potential for higher returns. Partnering with brick-and-mortar retailers can help extend the distribution footprint of the Dollar Shave Club (on the downside, the subscription model cannot readily be implemented in traditional retail stores). Developing and manufacturing its own shaving system can help Dollar Shave Club create its own unique offering (on the downside, this option requires a significant investment of resources).

Company Value Proposition

- Company value equation
  - *Benefits:* Generate profits (monetary benefits); gain market position, build a strong consumer brand, create loyal customer base (strategic benefits).
  - *Costs:* Communication and distribution expenses, cost of goods sold, general and administrative expenses (monetary costs).
- **Reason to invest:** Potential for exponential market growth and multifold return on investment.

Dollar Shave Club Company Offering

Offering	Features	Company value
Product	[Outlined in the customer value map]	*Benefits:* Creates competency in developing shaving products *Costs:* Cost of goods sold
Service	[Outlined in the customer value map]	*Benefits:* Develops and sustains customer relationships *Costs:* Service expenses
Brand	[Outlined in the customer value map]	*Benefits:* Builds brand equity *Costs:* Brand-building expenses
Price	[Outlined in the customer value map]	*Benefits:* Generates sales revenue *Costs:* Payment processing expenses (e.g., credit card fees)
Incentives	[Outlined in the customer value map]	*Benefits:* Promote consumer demand *Costs:* Incentive (free razor) expenses
Communication	[Outlined in the customer value map]	*Benefits:* Informs consumers about the offering and generates demand *Costs:* Communication expenses
Distribution	[Outlined in the customer value map]	*Benefits:* Makes product available to customers *Costs:* Website development and maintenance expenses, order fulfillment expenses, shipping expenses

WARBY PARKER:
BUILDING A LIFESTYLE BRAND

*It is not the strongest of the species that survives, nor the
most intelligent, but the one most responsive to change.*
—Charles Darwin, English naturalist and geologist

Warby Parker was founded in 2010 by four students—Neil Blumenthal, Andrew Hunt, David Gilboa, and Jeffrey Raider—in the MBA program at the Wharton School of the University of Pennsylvania.[7] Warby Parker provides high-quality eyeglasses at significantly lower prices than those of traditional designer brands. The company leverages e-commerce and employs a direct-to-consumer distribution model to eliminate much of the overhead involved in operating a brick-and-mortar eyewear store.

Warby Parker primarily sells eyewear online and maintains only a small number of showrooms located in boutiques throughout the United States. The company's home-try-on program allows customers to choose five frames from the website, which they receive to try at home for five days, free of charge. In addition, Warby Parker's website allows customers to use a webcam or upload a picture to virtually try on glasses.

Warby Parker uses a buy one, give one approach: For each pair of glasses purchased, it pays for the production of another pair of eyeglasses for someone in need. To accomplish this, Warby Parker partnered with nonprofit organizations that train men and women in developing countries to give basic eye exams and sell glasses to their communities at affordable prices.

The Warby Parker online store was launched in 2010. A month later it already had a waiting list of 20,000 customers. Warby Parker's business model and market success attracted a number of investors including Menlo Ventures Talent Capital, Spark Capital, American Express, Wellington Management, Tiger Global Management, General Catalyst Partners, and T. Rowe Price. In 2016, Warby Parker was valued at $1.2 billion after its last round of funding.

Warby Parker Market Value Map

Warby Parker's market value map delineates the target market, the company's offering in this market, and the ways in which this offering creates value for its target customers, its collaborators, and the company stakeholders.

Warby Parker Market Value Map

Target Market	Market Offering
Customers Individuals seeking reasonably priced designer eyeglasses; most fall in the 18–34 urban demographic	**Product** Eyeglasses with anti-reflective, polycarbonate prescription lenses. Initial product line includes 27 frame styles and one monocle
Collaborators Suppliers of raw materials, eyewear manufacturers, optical labs, logistics partners, boutique retailers	**Service** 30-day, no-questions-asked, free return policy; virtual try-on program; up to five frames shipped to a customer's home to try for five days
Company Warby Parker designs and distributes eyeglasses	**WARBY PARKER** — **Brand** Brand name: Warby Parker Brand associations: classic, American heritage design, social responsibility
Competitors Designer eyeglasses by Burberry, Gucci, Prada, Oliver Peoples, Persol, and other upscale brands	**Price** $95 retail, free shipping for all demos (in-home try-ons) and purchases
Context $16+ billion prescription eye care industry with profit margins reflecting 10 to 25 times markup	**Incentives** One-for-one donation, purchasing carbon credits to offset greenhouse gas emissions

Value Proposition	Market Offering (cont.)
Customer Value Stylish, affordable eyeglasses that customers can order online and try at home	**Communication** Press coverage, social media, banner advertising, keyword search, event marketing, WarbyParker.com
Collaborator Value Incremental revenues, incremental traffic, brand building, greater scope of operations	**Distribution** warbyparker.com website and nine Warby Parker showrooms for placing orders; UPS and FedEx for order delivery
Company Value Generate profits, gain market position, build a strong brand, create a loyal customer base, promote social responsibility	

Target Market

- **Customers**: Individuals seeking reasonably priced designer eyeglasses; most are in the 18–34 urban demographic.

- **Collaborators**: Raw material (cellulose acetate) supplier based in Italy, two manufacturers located in China, two optical labs based in New York; nine boutique eyeglass retailers serving as showrooms, a supply-chain management company (Navarre) handling order fulfillment and quality control, and a nonprofit organization (VisionSpring) implementing the one-for-one corporate social responsibility initiative.

- **Company**: Warby Parker is a designer and distributor of fashionable eyeglasses. Its core competency is in designing trendy eyewear, brand building, and direct-to-consumer distribution.

- **Competition**: High-end designer eyeglasses. Luxottica Group is the market leader in the U.S. brick-and-mortar retail eye care industry with 30% share; it manufactures eyewear for most fashion brands including Ralph Lauren, Chanel, Prada, Burberry, Gucci, Brooks Brothers, and Armani. Luxottica owns Oakley, Ray-Ban,

Oliver Peoples, and Persol brands, as well as the optical retail channels LensCrafters, Sunglass Hut, and Pearle Vision.

- Context: A $16+ billion prescription eye care industry with profit margins reflecting a markup of 10 to 25 times from point of manufacture to point of sale. Online shopping is gaining ground as many consumers have become accustomed to buying items over the Internet. Consumers, especially from younger demographics, are increasingly interested in having a social impact and making a difference in the world.

Value Proposition

- Customer value proposition: Stylish, competitively priced eyeglasses that customers can order online and try at home; enabling customers to contribute to an important social cause.

- Collaborator value proposition: Suppliers, manufacturers, and distributors receive incremental revenue by offering their products and services to Warby Parker. Retailers receive the additional benefit of offering a unique product that drives store traffic and enhances their brand. Corporate social responsibility partners benefit by expanding the scope of their activities.

- Company value proposition: Generate revenues and profits, gain market position, build a strong consumer brand, create a loyal customer base, and make the world a better place.

Market Offering

- Product: Eyeglasses with anti-reflective, polycarbonate prescription lenses. Initial product line includes 27 frame styles and one monocle.

- Service: A 30-day, no-questions-asked, free return policy; virtual try-on program; up to five frames shipped to a customer's home to try for five days; expert advice offered in retail boutiques.

- Brand: Warby Parker (combination of the names of Warby Pepper and Zagg Parker—fictitious characters created by American novelist Jack Kerouac). *Brand logo:* WARBY PARKER in capital letters. *Sub-brands:* Roosevelt, Huxley, Winston, Begley, etc., with each sub-brand corresponding to a specific eyewear style. *Key brand associations:* Classic American heritage design, exceptional value, outstanding customer service, and social responsibility.

- Price: $95 retail, free shipping for all demos (in-home try-ons) and purchases.

- Incentives: One-for-one donation (for every pair of glasses sold, the company pays to distribute a pair to someone in need); purchasing carbon credits to offset the greenhouse gas emissions produced through frame production, shipping, and warehousing to become carbon neutral.

- Communication: Press coverage (*GQ, Vogue, New York Times*); social media; online advertising on third-party websites; keyword search; event marketing (New York

Fashion Week and Art Basel Miami); advertising in retail outlets (boutique eyeglass stores); company website (WarbyParker.com).

- **Distribution:** WarbyParker.com website and nine Warby Parker showrooms for placing orders; UPS and FedEx for order delivery.

Warby Parker Customer Value Map

Target Customers

- **Customer needs:** Trendy, high-quality, reasonably priced eyeglasses; desire to contribute to society to make the world a better place.

- **Customer profile:** Young professionals wearing prescription eyeglasses.

Competition

- **Key competitors:** Eyeglasses by established prestige brands including Burberry, Gucci, Prada, Oliver Peoples, and Persol.

- **Competitor value proposition:** High-quality eyeglasses from a prestigious and reputable brand.

- **Attributes of the competitive offerings:** A pair of designer eyeglasses is typically priced between $300 and $800. Customers typically order and receive eyeglasses in a brick-and-mortar retail location. Some retailers offer while-you-wait service, whereas others require two separate visits to order and receive the eyeglasses.

Customer Value Proposition

- **Customer value equation**

  - *Benefits:* Trendy high-quality eyewear, easy ordering process (functional benefits); enables consumers to express their identity, style, creativity, and social responsibility (psychological benefits); lower price than those of traditional designer brands (monetary benefit).

  - *Costs:* Price paid for the eyeglasses (monetary cost); unproven product quality (functional cost), lesser known brand (psychological cost).

- **Competitive advantage**

  - *Points of dominance:* Low price, social purpose.
  - *Points of parity:* Design, frame, and lens quality.

- **Reason to choose:** Trendy fashion at a fraction of the price of traditional designer brands.

Warby Parker Customer Offering

Offering	Features	Customer Value
Product	Quality fashionable eyeglass frames in a variety of styles	Trendy eyeglasses that fit one's personality
	Anti-reflective, polycarbonate lenses	Increase vision clarity and reduce strain on eyes
Service	30-day, no-questions-asked free return policy	Reduces customer risk
	Home try-on program: up to five frames shipped to a customer's home to try for five days	Reduces customers' uncertainty about the eyewear fit; done in the convenience of one's home
	Virtual try-on program enabling customers to upload a photo and try on frames virtually	Reduces customers' uncertainty about eyewear aesthetics and fit; done instantly using a computer from any location
	Expert advice (offered in retail boutiques)	Reduces customers' uncertainty about the eyewear aesthetics and fit; offers expert advice
Brand	*Brand name:* Warby Parker	Creates unique brand identity; conveys creativity
	Logo: WARBY PARKER in capital letters	Conveys simplicity and style
	Sub-brands: Roosevelt, Huxley, Winston, Begley, etc., with each sub-brand corresponding to a specific eyewear style	Customers can think of anthropomorphized brands as people and find it easier to relate to these brands
	Key brand associations: Classic American heritage, exceptional value, outstanding customer service, social responsibility	Make the brand meaningful and relevant to its target customers
Price	$95	Cost to the customer is significantly lower than for traditional designer eyeglasses
	Free shipping	No extra shipping cost
Incentives	One-for-one donation: for every pair of glasses sold, the company pays to distribute a pair to someone in need	Satisfaction from contributing to an important social cause
	Purchasing carbon credits to offset the greenhouse gas emissions produced through frame production, shipping, and warehousing	Satisfaction from contributing to an important social cause

Communication	*Message:* Warby Parker is a fashion brand offering $95 prescription eyeglasses, delivering an outstanding experience, and having a social purpose	Communicates the key benefits and the essence of the Warby Parker brand and products
	Media: Press coverage (*GQ, Vogue, New York Times*); social media; online advertising; keyword search; event marketing (New York Fashion Week and Art Basel Miami); advertising in retail outlets; warbyparker.com	Broad range of media informs customers about the essence of the Warby Parker brand and the benefits of Warby Parker eyeglasses
	Creative format: Simple language and clean, stylish look and feel of all communications	Conveys clear brand message and easy-to-understand benefits
Distribution	Direct sales (ordered on warbyparker.com and delivered to customers by UPS or FedEx)	Offers convenient purchase process without having to visit a brick-and-mortar store
	Warby Parker showrooms (glasses ordered in showrooms and delivered by UPS or FedEx)	Enable customers to see, touch, and order the product

Warby Parker Collaborator Value Map

For brevity, the collaborator value map depicts only retailers; value maps for suppliers, manufacturers, and fulfillment centers follow a similar format.

Collaborators

- **Collaborator profile:** Nine boutique eyeglass retailers serving as Warby Parker showrooms.

- **Collaborator goals:** Increase sales revenues and profit by gaining access to new markets.

Competitive Offering

- **Key competitors:** Quality eyeglasses from established prestige brands including Burberry, Gucci, Prada, Oliver Peoples, and Persol.

- **Competitor value proposition:** Established brands with proven product quality, strong consumer demand, and high profit margins.

- **Attributes of the competitive offerings:** A pair of designer eyeglasses is typically priced between $300 and $800; retailers receive a percentage of the retail price. Most frames for fashion eyeglasses—including Ralph Lauren, Chanel, Prada, Oakley, Ray-Ban, Oliver Peoples, and Persol—are manufactured by Luxottica. Many of the lenses are supplied by Essilor International.

Collaborator Value Proposition

- Collaborator value equation
  - *Benefits:* Increases profits (monetary benefits); drives store traffic, broadens retailers' assortment by offering trendy fashion eyewear at a lower price point; enhances retailers' image by carrying a hip brand (strategic benefits).
  - *Costs:* Inventory costs, selling costs (monetary costs); opportunity costs of the retail space (strategic costs).
- Competitive advantage
  - *Points of dominance:* Appeals to a different customer segment; rent-plus-commission model guarantees steady revenues without an upfront capital investment.
  - *Point of parity:* Profitability.
  - *Points of compromise:* Unproven business model, uncertain customer demand, startup without established track record.
- **Reason to choose:** Low-risk opportunity to attract new customer segment.

Warby Parker Collaborator Offering

Offering	Features	Retailer value
Product	[Outlined in the customer value map]	Unique offering that drives store traffic
Service	[Outlined in the customer value map]	Unique offering that drives store traffic
	Training and support of sales associates	Trains sales associates and resolves problems faced by retailers
Brand	[Outlined in the customer value map]	Adds a trendy dimension to the retailer's brand; makes the retailer's price image more affordable
Price	Rent for hosting a showroom	Steady stream of revenue
	Sales commission for each pair of glasses sold at $95	Stream of performance-based revenue
Incentives	None	None
Communication	*Message:* Source of revenue and store traffic, broadens the store appeal by offering a hip, low-priced fashion option	Creates monetary and strategic value for the retailer
	Media: Personal sales	Informs retailers about the offering
Distribution	Products are procured by Navarre — the logistics company handling fulfillment	Reliable order fulfillment

Warby Parker Company Value Map

Company

- Company profile: Warby Parker designs and sells trendy eyeglasses. The company's core competency is in designing trendy eyewear, brand building, and direct-to-consumer distribution.

- Company goals: Generate revenues and profits (monetary goal); gain market position, build a strong consumer brand, create a loyal customer base, and make the world a better place (strategic goal).

Alternative Options

- Key alternatives: Investing in a different business model within the prescription eyewear industry or investing in a different industry altogether.

- Value proposition of the alternative options: Potential for higher monetary returns and greater social impact.

Company Value Proposition

- Company value equation
  - *Benefits:* Generate sales revenue and profits (monetary benefits); build strong brand, build a viable company, create societal value (strategic benefits).
  - *Costs:* Communication and distribution expenses, cost of goods sold, general and administrative expenses (monetary costs).

- **Reason to invest:** Potential for exponential market growth and multifold return on investment.

Warby Parker Company Offering

Offering	Features	Company value
Product	[Outlined in the customer and collaborator value maps]	*Benefits:* Developing competency in eyewear design *Costs:* R&D and production expenses
Service	[Outlined in the customer and collaborator value maps]	*Benefits:* Developing competency in service management *Costs:* R&D and service expenses
Brand	[Outlined in the customer value map]	*Benefits:* Creates brand equity that can be monetized *Costs:* Brand-building expenses
Price	[Outlined in the customer and collaborator value maps]	*Benefits:* Sales revenue *Costs:* Payment processing expenses (e.g., credit card fees)

Incentives	[Outlined in the customer and collaborator value maps]	*Benefits:* Promote consumer demand *Costs:* Incentives-related expenses
Communication	[Outlined in the customer and collaborator value maps]	*Benefits:* Informs consumers and retailers about the offering *Costs:* Communication expenses
Distribution	[Outlined in the customer and collaborator value maps]	*Benefits:* Delivers the eyeglasses directly to customers *Costs:* Logistics and shipping expenses, rent, sales commissions

NEST LABS:
DESIGNING THE CONNECTED HOME

*Design is not just what it looks like
and feels like. Design is how it works.*
—Steve Jobs, founder of Apple

Nest Labs develops programmable, self-learning, sensor-driven, Wi-Fi-enabled home automation devices that include thermostats, smoke detectors, and other security systems. Nest Labs was co-founded in 2010 by two former Apple engineers—Tony Fadell and Matt Rogers—who supervised the development of the iPod. The company's flagship product—Nest Learning Thermostat—was launched in October 2011.

Nest is an electronic, self-programmable, Wi-Fi-enabled thermostat using a machine-learning algorithm to detect consumer preferences and maintain the optimal temperature in their homes.

Round-shaped with a large high-resolution LCD display, the Nest thermostat offers a radically different way of programming compared to the other temperature-control devices on the market. Rather than presetting the daily and weekly temperatures for different time intervals throughout each day of the week—a daunting task for many consumers, who find it difficult to predict their future preferences—Nest tracks customers' actual behavior and uses it to predict their future preferences. Thus, for the first week users manually set the thermostat to their preferred temperature by spinning and clicking its control wheel (or using their smart phone or tablet), which enables the device to learn their schedule and desired temperatures. Using temperature and motion sensors, the Nest thermostat constantly monitors and, when necessary, modifies the programmed schedule.

By the end of 2013, Nest Labs had grown to nearly 300 employees and had sold over one million Nest thermostats in the United States. The company's rapid growth and market potential secured investments from a number of prominent venture capital firms including Kleiner Perkins Caufield & Byers, Google Ventures, Venrock, Shasta Ventures, Generation Capital, and Lightspeed Venture Partners. In January 2014, less than four years after Nest Labs was launched, it was acquired by Google (Alphabet Inc.) for US$3.2 billion.

Nest Market Value Map

The market value map delineates Nest's target market, its offering in this market, and the ways in which this offering creates value for its target customers, collaborators, and company stakeholders.

Nest Market Value Map

Target Market	Market Offering
Customers People who seek to control the temperature in their homes for optimal comfort and low energy usage	**Product** Programmable Wi-Fi thermostat featuring large, round-shaped LCD display
Collaborators Retailers, contractors installing the thermostat, and new construction developers	**Service** Auto-scheduling/auto-away functionality supported by 24/7 customer service
Company Nest Labs—a home automation company producing learning, sensor-driven, Wi-Fi-enabled devices	**Brand** Brand name: Nest Brand associations: energy savings and convenience; Brand motto: "The brighter way to save energy" **nest**
Competitors Thermostats manufactured by companies such as Honeywell, Emerson, Broan, Lux, and White-Rodgers	**Price** $249 (suggested retail price) $149–$199 (wholesale price)
Context Increasing consumer interest in environmentally friendly technologies and a "connected home"	**Incentives** $50 instant discount from Nest Up to $100 rebate from local utilities
Value Proposition	**Communication** Banner advertising, keyword search, in-store displays, targeted emails, product packaging, Nest.com
Customer Value Energy savings, reduced environmental impact, greater comfort, aesthetic appeal, easy setup	**Distribution** Direct sales (Nest.com), online retailers (Amazon.com), brick-and-mortar retailers (Home Depot, Walmart)
Collaborator Value Generate profits and store traffic (retailers), increase workload (contractors); increase profits (developers)	
Company Value Generate profits, gain market position, build a strong brand, and create a loyal customer base	

Target Market

- **Customers:** Homeowners and homebuyers who seek a simple way to remotely control the temperature in their homes for optimal comfort and low energy usage.

- **Collaborators:** Retailers, contractors installing the thermostat, and new construction developers.

- **Company:** Nest Labs is a home automation company producing programmable, self-learning, sensor-driven, Wi-Fi-enabled devices. Its core competency is in home automation, customer-centric product design, and machine learning.

- **Competition:** Thermostats manufactured by companies such as Honeywell (the market leader), Emerson, Broan, Lux, and White-Rodgers.

- Context: Growing consumer interest in environmentally friendly technologies, growing adoption of internet-connected devices, technological advances in machine learning and the Internet of Things, government-sponsored energy-efficiency incentives and rebates.

Value Proposition

- Customer value proposition: Energy savings, reduced environmental impact, greater comfort, aesthetic appeal, easy programming.

- Collaborator value proposition: Generate profits and drive store traffic (retailers); generate profits and increase workload by obtaining additional projects (contractors); increase profits (developers).

- Company value proposition: Generate revenues and profits (monetary goal); gain market position, establish Nest Labs as a key player in the Internet of Things for home automation, build a strong consumer brand, and create a loyal customer base (strategic goal).

Market Offering

- Product: Programmable Wi-Fi thermostat featuring large, round-shaped LCD display.

- Service: Auto-scheduling/auto-away functionality supported by 24/7 customer service.

- Brand: Nest. *Brand logo:* "nest" in gray lower case. *Brand motto:* "The brighter way to save energy." *Key brand associations:* Learning thermostat, comfort, technology, connected home. **nest**

- Price: $249 (MSRP); $149–$199 wholesale price.

- Incentives: $50 instant discount from Nest and up to $100 rebate from local utilities.

- Communication: Social media, press coverage, product packaging, printed materials included with the product (welcome guide), in-store displays, advertising, keyword search, targeted emails, company website (Nest.com).

- Distribution: Direct sales (Nest.com), online retailers (Amazon.com), and brick-and-mortar retailers (Home Depot, Walmart).

Nest Customer Value Map

Target Customers

- Customer needs: A simple way to remotely control the temperature at home for optimal comfort and low energy usage.

- Customer profile

- *Do-it-yourself homeowners* who buy the thermostat from retail stores and install it themselves.

- *Full-service homeowners* who use a contractor to install the thermostat and buy the thermostat from the contractor.

- *Homebuyers* who purchase a newly constructed property with an installed thermostat chosen by the developer.

Competition

- **Key competitors**

  - *Traditional non-programmable, non-web-enabled thermostats* manufactured by companies such as Honeywell, Emerson, Broan, and Lux.

  - *Programmable, non-web-enabled thermostats* manufactured by companies such as Honeywell, Emerson, and Lux.

  - *Programmable Wi-Fi thermostats* manufactured by companies such as Honeywell, Ecobee, Emerson, and Lux.

- **Competitor value proposition**

  - *Traditional non-programmable, non-web-enabled thermostats* are inexpensive, easy to install, and easy to operate (benefits) but are not energy efficient (costs).

  - *Programmable, non-web-enabled thermostats* are moderately priced, are relatively easy to install, and are energy efficient (benefits) but are often difficult to operate (costs).

  - *Programmable Wi-Fi thermostats* are energy efficient (benefit) but are relatively expensive and could be difficult to install and operate (costs).

Customer Value Proposition

- **Customer value equation**

  - *Benefits:* Greater comfort (functional benefit), satisfaction from having an environmentally friendly and aesthetically appealing device (psychological benefit), energy savings (monetary benefit).

  - *Costs:* Effort involved in replacing the thermostat (functional cost), mental effort in learning how to operate the thermostat (psychological cost), price paid to buy and install the thermostat (monetary cost).

- **Competitive advantage**

  - *Points of dominance:* Ability of device to self-learn (primary benefit), energy savings (primary benefit relative to traditional thermostats), ease of use, and aesthetic appeal.

- *Points of parity:* Energy savings (relative to smart thermostats), remote control (relative to smart Wi-Fi thermostats), ease of installation (relative to traditional thermostats).
- *Point of compromise:* Price.
- **Reason to choose**: Easy programming and energy savings.

Nest Customer Offering

Offering	Features	Customer value
Product	Compatible with 95% of 24V heating and cooling systems	Compatible with customers' current heating and cooling systems
	3.3" (diameter) by 1.2" (depth) shape with rounded edges in stainless steel	Unobtrusive yet large enough to be easy to read and operate; conveys high-tech look and feel
	Temperature, humidity, light, near-field and far-field activity sensors	Product features necessary to enable the learning (auto-scheduling and auto-away)
	Includes optional trim kit, mounting screws, wiring labels, and a screwdriver	Simplifies the installation process by including all necessary components
	Two-year limited warranty	Signals reliability and offers customers peace of mind
Service	Nest phone/tablet app	User-friendly interface enabling consumers to remotely set and monitor temperature at home
	Auto-schedule	Nest learns the temperatures customers prefer and programs itself in about a week
	Auto-away	Nest automatically turns itself down when customers are away from home to help save energy
	24/7 phone and online technical support	Addresses potential problems in installing and using the thermostat
Brand	*Name:* Nest	Conveys comfort and safety
	Logo: The word *nest* in gray lower case Akkurat font	Conveys high-tech image
	Motto: The brighter way to save energy	Communicates the main function of the thermostat: energy savings
	Key brand associations: Learning thermostat, comfort, technology, connected home	Make the brand meaningful and relevant to its target customers

Price	$249 MSRP (manufacturer suggested retail price)	Cost to the customer The price is higher than that of traditional thermostats
Incentives	$50 instant discount offered by Nest	Lowers the purchase price without additional effort on the part of buyers
	$20–$100 rebate offered by local utilities	Lowers the purchase price; requires customers to fill in and submit a rebate form
Communication	*Message:* A home that takes care of the people inside it and the world around it	Communicates the key benefit (energy savings), promising a simple and meaningful experience
	Media: Social media, press coverage, product packaging, printed materials included with the product, in-store displays, Nest.com website, advertising on third-party websites, keyword search, targeted emails	Broad range of media informs customers about the benefits of Nest thermostats
	Creative format: Simple language, clean, Apple-like look and feel of all communications (ads, product displays, installation and usage guides, packaging)	Easy-to-understand product benefits, installation instructions, and user guide
Distribution	Direct sales (Nest.com)	Offers detailed installation, use, and support information
	Online retailers (Amazon.com)	Easy purchase option for customers with an existing account
	Brick-and-mortar retailers: hardware stores (Home Depot), mass-merchandisers (Walmart), electronics stores (Best Buy)	Enable customers to see, touch, and purchase the product

Nest Collaborator Value Map

Collaborators

- Retailers

    - *Profile:* Online retailers (Amazon.com), hardware stores (Home Depot), mass-merchandisers (Walmart), and numerous small retailer outlets.

    - *Goals:* Generate profits; drive store traffic.

- Contractors

  - *Profile:* Electricians, heating and air-conditioning contractors, and general contractors.

  - *Goals:* Generate profits by increasing workload and margins.

- Developers

  - *Profile:* Residential and office building developers.

  - *Goals:* Generate profits by enhancing the value of the development.

Competition

- Key competitors

  - *Traditional non-programmable, non-web-enabled thermostats* manufactured by companies such as Honeywell, Emerson, Broan, and Lux.

  - *Programmable, non-web-enabled thermostats* manufactured by companies such as Honeywell, Emerson, and Lux.

  - *Programmable Wi-Fi thermostats,* manufactured by companies such as Honeywell, Ecobee, Emerson, and Lux.

- Competitor value proposition

  - *Traditional non-programmable, non-web-enabled thermostats* are inexpensive and easy to install (benefits) but offer relatively low profit margins (costs).

  - *Programmable, non-web-enabled thermostats* are moderately priced and are relatively easy to install (benefits) but are a declining category as an increasing number of customers prefer Wi-Fi thermostats (costs).

  - *Programmable Wi-Fi thermostats* are in demand by customers and are higher margin products (benefits) but are relatively expensive and more difficult to install (costs).

Collaborator Value Proposition: Retailers

- Collaborator value equation

  - *Benefits:* Additional source of revenue and profit (monetary benefits); drives store traffic, enhances retailers' image (strategic benefits).

  - *Costs:* Inventory costs, selling costs, opportunity cost of the retail space (monetary costs).

- Competitive advantage

  - *Points of dominance:* Customer demand (generated by Nest's promotional activities), trade incentives, profit margins (compared to traditional thermostats).
  - *Point of parity:* Profit margins.

- *Point of compromise:* Risk associated with selling an unknown brand from a company without an established track record.

- **Reason to choose**: Trade incentives (source of revenues) and customer demand (store traffic).

Collaborator Value Proposition: Contractors

- **Collaborator value equation**

  - *Benefits:* Additional source of revenues and profits (monetary benefits); generates new customers/projects, greater customer satisfaction from larger assortment of thermostat options (strategic benefits).

  - *Costs:* Inventory costs of carrying an additional product, time value of learning to install Nest products (monetary costs); endorsing a product without a proven reliability track record (strategic costs).

- **Competitive advantage**

  - *Points of dominance:* Customer demand (generated by Nest's promotional activities), ease of installation.
  - *Point of parity:* Price (compared to other smart Wi-Fi thermostats).
  - *Points of compromise:* Lack of professional version available exclusively for contractors (which would give higher margins to contractors), lack of reliability track record.

- **Reason to choose**: Increases customer satisfaction by offering a greater variety of options.

Collaborator Value Proposition: Developers

- **Collaborator value equation**

  - *Benefits:* Ability to charge higher prices for finished construction due to a price premium for a connected home built into the development price (monetary benefit); increased consumer interest in a connected home can drive traffic (strategic benefit).

  - *Costs:* Cost of the thermostat, time value of learning to install Nest products (monetary costs); using a product without a proven reliability track record, unproven demand across different customer segments (strategic costs).

- **Competitive advantage**

  - *Point of dominance:* Customer appeal.
  - *Points of parity:* Installation cost, technical support.
  - *Points of compromise:* Price, risk associated with the fact that the company and the product do not have an established track record.

- **Reason to choose**: Increases appeal of the development, enabling the developer to demand a higher price.

Nest Collaborator Offering[8]

Offering	Features	Retailer value
Product	[Outlined in the customer value map]	Generates customer demand
	RFID tag	Helps reduce product theft in brick-and-mortar stores
Service	[Outlined in the customer value map]	Generates customer demand
	Inventory monitoring	Facilitates managing retail inventory to ensure product availability
	Reverse logistics (return processing)	Facilitates processing of customer returns
	Phone and online sales support	Offers information and resolves problems faced by retailers
Brand	[Outlined in the customer value map]	Nest brand is recognizable by customers and facilitates interest
Price	60%–80% of $249 (40%–20% retail margin)	Stream of revenue
	Prepayment discount	Discount for prepayment lowers the price paid by the retailer
Incentives	Slotting allowance	Payment for including the product in the retailer's inventory
	Advertising allowance	Payment for promoting a product
	Breakage (slippage) allowance	Payment offered to retailers to cover product returns and return logistics
Communication	*Message:* High-margin product sought by consumers, supported by large communication campaign	Generates retailer revenues and profit; drives store traffic
	Media: Trade press, trade shows, and direct sales	Provides retailers with information about the offering
	Creative format: Simple language, clean look and feel, streamlined communications	Conveys easy-to-understand benefits
Distribution	Direct distribution	Larger retailers can procure the product directly from Nest.com
	Wholesaler distribution	Smaller retailers can procure the product from wholesalers

Nest Company Value Map

The Company

- **Company Profile:** Nest Labs is a home automation company with a core competency in home automation and customer-centric product design.
- **Company goals:** Generate revenues and profits (monetary goal); gain market position, establish Nest Labs as a key player in the Internet of Things for home automation, build a strong brand, and create a loyal customer base (strategic goal).

Alternative Options

- **Key alternatives:** Investing in different home automation devices such as smoke detectors, security cameras, door locks, doorbells, security systems, and lighting.
- **Value proposition of the alternative options:** Potential for higher revenues and profits.

Company Value Proposition

- **Company value equation**

  - *Benefits:* Sales revenues and profits (monetary benefits); creation of a technological platform (ecosystem) for developing a line of networked products and services for the connected home, gathering of usage data to understand customer needs to optimize existing offerings and develop new ones, building a consumer brand, creating societal value by promoting energy-efficient products (strategic benefits).

  - *Costs:* Research and development expenses, service and support costs, communication and distribution expenses, cost of goods sold, general and administrative expenses (monetary costs).

- **Reason to invest:** Nest thermostat is a high-margin offering that can establish Nest Labs as a key player in the Internet of Things for home automation.

Nest Company Offering

Offering	Features	Company value
Product	[Outlined in the customer and collaborator value maps]	*Benefits:* Develops a platform for connected home products such as smoke alarms and security cameras *Costs:* R&D and manufacturing expenses
Service	[Outlined in the customer and collaborator value maps]	*Benefits:* Develops a platform for connected home services such as smoke alarm and security camera monitoring *Costs:* R&D and service expenses

Brand	[Outlined in the customer value map]	*Benefits:* Creates brand equity that can be monetized
		Costs: Brand-building expenses
Price	[Outlined in the customer and collaborator value maps]	*Benefits:* Sales revenue
		Costs: Payment processing expenses
Incentives	[Outlined in the customer and collaborator value maps]	*Benefits:* Promote consumer demand and motivate retailers to push the product
		Costs: Incentive expenses
Communication	[Outlined in the customer and collaborator value maps]	*Benefits:* Informs consumers and retailers about the offering
		Costs: Communication expenses
Distribution	[Outlined in the customer and collaborator value maps]	*Benefits:* Makes the product available to customers
		Costs: Product delivery expenses, fulfillment expenses (direct sales), trade margins and incentives (sales via retailers)

UBER:
CREATING THE PERFECT RIDE

Everything you can imagine is real.
— Pablo Picasso, Spanish painter and sculptor

U ber was founded in 2009 by Travis Kalanick and Garrett Camp. Initially named UberCab, the company was renamed Uber in 2011 because it was not licensed to operate a taxi service. Headquartered in San Francisco, Uber connects individuals needing a ride with freelance drivers willing to drive them to their destination.

Originally a black-car service (now UberBlack), over the next five years Uber introduced a range of services including UberX, a low-cost service using regular cars; UberCab, a low-cost service using the existing network of taxis; UberPool, a ride-sharing service; and UberSelect, a premium service using luxury cars. In addition to passenger rides, Uber introduced a variety of additional services including UberRush, a bicycle delivery service in heavily populated metropolitan areas; UberCargo, a freight delivery service; and UberEats, an on-demand food-delivery service.

Uber's business model attracted a wide range of investors including venture firms First Round Capital, Google Ventures, Menlo Ventures, Goldman Sachs, and Benchmark Capital; car manufacturers like General Motors, Volkswagen, and Toyota; and individual investors like Amazon founder Jeff Bezos, AngelList founder Naval Ravikant, and Yelp cofounder Jeremy Stoppelman.

Uber went live in June 2010 in San Francisco and in 2011 in New York. In 2013 it was launched in London and in 2014 made its debut in China. By 2016, Uber had achieved two billion rides, raised over $12 billion in capital, and reached an implied valuation of $66 billion, making it the highest valued startup in the world.

Uber Market Value Map

Uber's market value map delineates the target market, the company's offering in this market, and the ways in which this offering creates value for target customers, collaborators, and company stakeholders.

Uber Market Value Map

Target Market

Customers
Individuals needing fast, convenient, reliable, comfortable, and inexpensive transportation

Collaborators
Independent drivers, black-car service companies, mapping services, car manufacturers; financial institutions

Company
Uber is a transportation network company with a competency in logistics and managing customer networks

Competitors
Traditional taxi services and other ridesharing services including Lyft, Curb, Grab, Gett, and MyTaxi

Context
Inefficient taxi/limo industry, smartphone penetration, advances in GPS technology, regulatory hurdles

Value Proposition

Customer Value
Fast, convenient, reliable, comfortable, and inexpensive transportation

Collaborator Value
Source of income, flexible working schedule, easy startup process

Company Value
Generate profits, gain market position, build a strong brand, and create a loyal customer base

Market Offering

Product
Uber mobile app

Service
Ridesharing (UberPool), regular car (UberX), large car (UberXL), taxi (UberCab), luxury car (UberSelect), black car (UberBlack)

Brand
Brand name: Uber
Brand associations: Fast, convenient ride (riders), extra income, flexible time (drivers)

Price
The price depends on the type of car service, distance, travel time, waiting time, customer demand, and local taxes

Incentives
First-time rider bonus ($5–$50); Driver sign-up bonus ($100–$500)

Communication
Television, outdoor and online advertising; press coverage; social media; keyword search, Uber.com

Distribution
Uber app is available online and Uber services are available in most major cities around the world

Target Market

- **Customers:** Individuals needing fast, convenient, reliable, comfortable, and value-priced transportation.

- **Collaborators:** Independent drivers; black-car and limo-service companies; mapping services including Google Maps; car manufacturers including General Motors, Volkswagen, and Toyota; financial institutions including Amex, Citibank, and Capital One; and hotel chains including Starwood, Hilton and IHG Hotels.

- **Company:** Uber is a transportation network company with a core competency in logistics and developing and managing platforms that connect customers with service providers.

- **Competition:** Traditional taxi services and other ridesharing services including Lyft, Curb, Grab, Gett, and MyTaxi.

- **Context:** The ubiquity of smartphones and advancements in GPS technology enable Uber to locate individuals needing a ride. An increasing number of regulations imposed by local authorities, including fingerprint background checks for drivers, is a challenge for Uber's business model.

Value Proposition

- **Customer value proposition:** Fast, convenient, reliable, comfortable, and inexpensive transportation.

- **Collaborator value proposition:** Source of income, flexible working schedule, easy startup process.

- **Company value proposition:** Generate revenues and profits, gain market position, build a strong consumer brand, and create a loyal customer base.

Market Offering

- **Product:** Uber mobile app

- **Service:** Ridesharing (UberPool), regular car (UberX), large car (UberXL), taxi (UberCab), luxury car (UberSelect), black car (UberBlack).

- **Brand:** Uber; stems from the German word *über* meaning "super." *Brand logo:* a square embedded in a circle (rider logo); a square embedded in a hexagon (driver logo). *Brand associations:* Fast and convenient transportation (for riders); source of extra income with a flexible schedule (for drivers).

- **Price:** The price of a ride depends on the type of car service, distance, travel time, waiting time, customer demand (surge pricing), and local taxes. Drivers receive a percentage of the price paid by customers.

- **Incentives:** First-time rider bonus ($5–$50); driver sign-up bonus ($100–$500).

- **Communication:** Television, outdoor, and online advertising; press coverage; social media; shared experiences; company website (Uber.com).

- **Distribution:** Uber app is available online; Uber services are available in most major cities around the world.

Uber Customer Value Map

Target Customers

- **Customer needs:** Fast, convenient, reliable, comfortable, and value-priced transportation.

- **Customer profile:** Individuals who do not own a car and/or have no driver's license; those having a night out, going to a party or a special event; business travelers and tourists.

Competition

- **Key competitors:** Traditional taxi services and other ridesharing services including Lyft, Curb, Grab, Gett, and MyTaxi.

- **Competitor value proposition:** Taxis, a traditional form of ride-for-hire, can be hailed on the street without a pre-order, do not require having a credit card, and employ full-time drivers familiar with local traffic. The other ridesharing services are generally at parity with Uber and vary in driver availability and price.

- **Attributes of the competitive offerings:** Taxis are centrally dispatched and managed, the fare is determined at the completion of the ride, drivers are accustomed to a tip that in many locations averages 15%, payments can be made in cash or with credit card, the number of taxis is regulated, and most taxi companies have apps enabling ordering online.

Customer Value Proposition

- **Customer value equation**

  - *Benefits:* Streamlined ordering process, reduced waiting time, comfortable ride, easy payment process (functional benefits); peace of mind because of reduced uncertainty about price, wait time, and destination arrival time (psychological benefits); lower price than a regular taxi (monetary benefit).

  - *Costs:* Price paid for the ride (monetary cost).

- **Competitive advantage**

  - *Points of dominance:* Convenience, availability, wait time, price.

  - *Points of parity:* Transportation for hire, duration of the ride.

- **Reason to choose:** More convenient, faster, and less expensive than taxis.

Uber Customer Offering

Offering	Features	Customer Value
Product	Uber rider app	Enables customers to manage the trip
Service	Ridesharing (UberPool), regular car (UberX), large car (UberXL), taxi (UberCab), luxury car (UberSelect), black car (UberBlack)	Provides customers with a variety of options to choose from depending on their needs
	Provides the rider with the location of the car, estimated time of arrival, and driver information	Reduces rider's uncertainty
	Provides the driver with rider's location and route	Simplifies order placement

Brand	*Brand name:* Uber (from the German *über*, meaning "super")	Creates distinct identity; conveys superior experience
	Logo: A square embedded in a circle	Conveys Uber's vision of "moving bits and atoms"
	Sub-brands: UberX, UberXL, UberSelect, UberCab, UberBlack, UberPool	Identify different types of Uber services
	Key brand associations: Convenient transportation; a cross between functionality and lifestyle	Convey the essence of the Uber brand
Price	The price of a ride depends on the type of service, distance, travel time, waiting time, customer demand, and local taxes	Cost to the customer Uber prices are typically lower than those of the competition
	The price is billed directly to the credit card on file (cash payments are not accepted)	Fast and easy payment format eliminates the need to carry cash
Incentives	First-time rider bonus (up to $50)	Reduces cost of trying Uber
Communication	*Message:* Fast, convenient, reliable transportation	Informs customers about Uber's benefits
	Media: Television, outdoor, and online advertising; press coverage; social media; shared experiences; company website	Broad range of media informs customers about Uber services
	Creative format: Clean look and feel. Taglines: "Everyone's private driver," "Ready anywhere, anytime," "Arrive in style"	Translates Uber's value proposition into a language that customers can easily understand and relate to
Distribution	Uber app available online	Enables customers to easily download the Uber app
	Uber services available in most major cities around the world	Uber services are available for most destinations

Uber Collaborator Value Map

For brevity, the collaborator value map depicts only independent drivers; value maps for other collaborators follow a similar format.

Collaborators

- Collaborator profile: Individuals who own or lease a car, need an additional source of income, and are willing to work as drivers.
- Collaborator goals: Additional source of income, flexible working hours.

Competition

- **Key competitors**: Traditional taxi services and other ridesharing services including Lyft, Curb, Grab, Gett, and MyTaxi (the analysis below focuses on the traditional taxi services).

- **Competitor value proposition**: Lower startup costs: drivers do not need to own their own car. The number of cabs in most locations is regulated, curbing the competition among cab drivers. Many customers are accustomed to the traditional taxi services.

- **Attributes of the competitive offerings**: Taxi drivers typically lease cabs maintained by companies that have purchased the right (medallion) to operate a certain number of taxis in a given area. Drivers' pay consists of the fares and tips they generate less the cab-leasing fee and cost of gas.

Collaborator Value Proposition

- **Collaborator value equation**

  - *Benefits:* Source of income (monetary benefit); flexible working schedule, easy startup process (functional benefits); sense of being one's own boss (psychological benefit).

  - *Costs:* Gasoline, car maintenance, insurance, income tax (monetary costs).

- **Competitive advantage**

  - *Points of dominance:* Flexible working hours, easier startup.
  - *Point of parity:* Overall pay (after taking expenses into account).
  - *Points of compromise:* Must own a car, tipping is not a standard practice.

- **Reason to choose**: Additional income with flexible schedule.

Uber Collaborator Offering

Offering	Features	Collaborator value
Product	Uber driver app	Enables drivers to manage the trip
Service	Connecting drivers with consumers in need of a ride	Provides customer traffic
	Provides the driver with customer's destination	Streamlines the car-hire process and saves time
	Destination route mapping	Optimizes the route and saves time
	Customer fare collection	Streamlines the payment process
Brand	*Brand name:* Uber	Creates a distinct brand identity
	Logo: A square embedded in a hexagon	Conveys the essence of Uber's vision of "moving bits and atoms"
	Associations: Fast and convenient transportation	Credibility stemming from the association with Uber

Price	Percentage (about 80%) of the customer fare	Source of income for the driver
	Driver payments can be disbursed daily	Speeds up access to earned money
Incentives	Sign-up bonus (up to $500)	Facilitates attracting new drivers
Communication	*Message:* Additional income and flexible work hours	Informs drivers about benefits of working for Uber
	Media: Television, outdoor advertisements, press coverage, social media, online advertising, word of mouth, uber.com website	Broad range of media informs potential drivers about Uber
	Creative format: Taglines: "Make extra money with your car," "Choose your hours, drive your own car, be your own boss, and make money"	Translates Uber's value proposition into a language that drivers can easily understand and relate to
Distribution	Uber app available online	Enables drivers to easily download the Uber app
	Uber services available in most major cities around the world	Driving for Uber is an option for many individuals seeking additional income

Uber Company Value Map

Company

- Company profile: Uber is a transportation network company with a core competency in logistics and developing and managing platforms for connecting customers with service providers.

- Company goals: Generate revenues and profits (monetary goal); gain market position, build a strong consumer brand, and create a loyal customer base (strategic goal).

Alternative Options

- Key alternatives: Investing in a different business model within the transportation industry or investing in a different industry altogether.

- Value proposition of the alternative options: Potential for higher monetary return on investment.

Company Value Proposition

- **Company value equation**

    - *Benefits:* Commissions on rides (monetary benefits); developing a technological platform and know-how for a broad range of transportation services (strategic benefits).

    - *Costs:* Research and development costs, service and support expenses, cost of driver and rider incentives, cost of advertising, legal expenses, general and administrative expenses (monetary costs).

- **Reason to invest:** Potential for exponential market growth and multifold return on investment.

Uber Company Offering

Offering	Features	Company value
Product	[Outlined in the customer and collaborator value maps]	*Benefits:* Uber app is an effective tool for connecting riders with drivers *Costs:* Development, upgrade, and maintenance costs
Service	[Outlined in the customer and collaborator value maps]	*Benefits:* Creates customer and driver loyalty *Costs:* Development, upgrade, and maintenance costs
Brand	[Outlined in the customer and collaborator value maps]	*Benefits:* Creates brand equity that can be monetized *Costs:* Brand-building expenses
Price	[Outlined in the customer and collaborator value maps]	*Benefits:* Sales revenue *Costs:* Payment processing expenses
Incentives	[Outlined in the customer and collaborator value maps]	*Benefits:* Generate rider demand and ensure supply of drivers *Costs:* Incentives-related expenses
Communication	[Outlined in the customer and collaborator value maps]	*Benefits:* Informs riders and drivers about the benefits of Uber *Costs:* Communication expenses
Distribution	[Outlined in the customer and collaborator value maps]	*Benefits:* Makes Uber app and services available to riders and drivers *Costs:* Cost of entering new markets and growing existing ones

ZENEFITS:
MANAGING EMPLOYEE BENEFITS
FOR THE SMALL BUSINESS

Success is a science; if you have the conditions, you get the result.
—Oscar Wilde, Irish playwright, novelist, and poet

Z enefits is a San Francisco-based business-to-business startup launched in 2013. The company aimed to streamline and automate the process by which small businesses buy and manage health insurance benefits for their employees.

Zenefits used the complexity and inefficiency of the traditional health brokerage market to its advantage by developing cloud-based software that automated the process of matching employers with the right insurance plan. To make its offering attractive to small businesses, Zenefits bundled the management of health insurance policies with a number of additional services designed to simplify human resource management—including payroll management; employee benefits management; tracking employee work time, vacation, and attendance; stock options administration; compensation/retirement planning and administration; and employee onboarding.[9] Zenefits offered all of its services to small businesses for free because the recurring monthly commissions from the health insurance policies were more than enough to make Zenefits profitable.

The company's market potential and rapid growth helped Zenefits secure funding from a number of seasoned venture capital funds including Andreessen Horowitz, Maverick Capital, Venrock, TPG, IVP, Khosla Ventures, and Fidelity Investments. In its very first year of operation, Zenefits signed up 2,000 small businesses with a combined 50,000 workers. The following year, Zenefits topped Forbes' 2014 hottest startup list, edging out Uber, Airbnb, and Lyft. During the same year, Zenefits was identified as one of the fastest growing software-as-a-service (SaaS) companies in history. A year later, Zenefits had reached a $4.5 billion valuation at its most recent round of funding.[10]

Zenefits Market Value Map

The Zenefits market value map delineates the target market, the company's offering in this market, and the ways in which this offering creates value for its target customers, its collaborators, and the company stakeholders.

Zenefits Market Value Map

Target Market		Market Offering	
Customers Small businesses with 5–200 employees		**Product** Zenefits offers its software as a service; there is no actual product that customers acquire rights to	
Collaborators Health insurance providers Specialized employee benefit providers		**Service** Streamlined benefit plan selection, administration of employee benefits, payroll, employee stock options, and retirement planning	
Company Zenefits—provider of cloud-based employee benefit solutions to small businesses		⚑ **ZENEFITS** — **Brand** Brand name: Zenefits; Brand associations: Easy management of employee benefits	
Competitors Traditional insurance brokers Online insurance broker services		**Price** Free to customers, Monthly commission (4%–8%) from insurance providers per insured employee for the duration of the policy	
Context $18 billion market; inefficient market lacking transparency; the Affordable Care Act adds complexity		**Incentives** None	
Value Proposition		**Communication** Personal sales, press coverage, social media, keyword search, online advertising, Zenefits.com	
Customer Value Streamlined benefit management at no additional cost			
Collaborator Value Additional channel to promote collaborator offerings		**Distribution** Cloud-based service available via zenefits.com	
Company Value Generate profits, gain market position, build a strong brand, and create a loyal customer base			

Target Market

- **Customers:** Small businesses that employ between 5 and 200 people.

- **Collaborators:** Health insurance providers including Kaiser Permanente, Aetna, and Anthem Blue Cross; specialized retirement benefit services, including employee option- and stock-management tool eShares and payroll provider Gusto.

- **Company:** Zenefits is a software company providing employee benefit solutions to small businesses. Its core competency is in software development and personal selling.

- **Competition:** Services offered by traditional insurance brokers and online insurance brokers including Oracle, Kronos, BenefitsConnect, and Epicor.

- **Context:** The health insurance brokerage market is estimated at $18 billion. Insurance brokers receive between 4% and 8% monthly commission for each insured employee for the duration of the policy. The Affordable Care Act, signed into law in 2010, introduced a number of new health care rules, including the requirements that health insurance providers publish set rates and that businesses with more than 50 employees must provide insurance to their workers.

Value Proposition

- Customer value proposition: Streamlined management of employee benefits at no additional cost.
- Collaborator value proposition: An alternative channel to reach customers.
- Company value proposition: Generate profits, gain market position, and create a loyal customer base.

Market Offering

- Product: Zenefits offers its software as a service; the offering does not involve an actual product that customers acquire the rights to.
- Service: Zenefits' core service streamlines the management of employee benefits for small businesses by facilitating selection of the optimal employee benefit and payroll plans; by compliance training and certification; by providing up-to-the-minute access to employee benefit information; and by enabling customers to set up, configure, and customize their benefits. Zenefits also offers web-based, email, and live customer support through a dedicated account team of advisors.
- Brand: Zenefits. *Brand logo:* A stylized bird next to the word "ZENEFITS," written in capital letters. *Brand associations:* Streamlined management of employee benefits.
- Price: Free.
- Incentives: None.
- Communication: Personal sales, press coverage, social media, online advertising, keyword search, company website (Zenefits.com).
- Distribution: Cloud-based service accessible though Zenefits.com website.

Zenefits Customer Value Map

Target Customers

- Customer needs: Small businesses that do not have a dedicated human resources department and seek a simple solution to manage employee benefits.
- Customer profile: Small businesses that employ between 5 and 200 people.

Competition

- Key competitors: Traditional insurance brokers.
- Competitor value proposition: Variety of insurance plans offered, in-person advice to help select the optimal benefit plan.
- Attributes of the competitive offerings: The traditional enrollment process involves filing signed paperwork for enrolled employees each time that something changes within an individual employee's plan. The offerings limited to health insurance coverage lack more comprehensive benefit management options such as employee payroll, stock option, and retirement administration assistance.

Customer Value Proposition

- Customer value equation

    - *Benefits:* Saves money on human resource management (monetary benefit); saves management time; improves accuracy, transparency, and compliance; streamlines onboarding and offboarding; gives peace of mind to companies inexperienced in human resource management (strategic benefits).

    - *Costs:* Risk of mismanaging employee benefits, monetary value of the time to learn to use Zenefits system (monetary costs).

- Competitive advantage

    - *Point of dominance:* More comprehensive benefit management (health care, payroll, stock options, and retirement administration).

    - *Points of parity:* Same portfolio of insurance plans as traditional brokers; broker services are free for the client.

    - *Point of compromise:* Lack of a personal interaction when choosing a benefit plan.

- **Reason to choose:** More comprehensive benefit management system at no additional cost.

Zenefits Customer Offering

Offering	Features	Customer Value
Product	None	—
Service	Matching employer needs with the available benefit plans	Efficient and cost-effective selection of the optimal plans
	Streamlined administration of employee benefits, payroll, employee stock options, retirement planning	Saves management time; improves accuracy, transparency, compliance; streamlines onboarding and offboarding
	Employee portal for managing benefit options and updating personal information	Saves management time and improves accuracy and transparency
	Automated web-based support combined with live support via phone/email	Offers training on using the system and addresses potential service-related issues
Brand	*Brand name:* Zenefits	Distinct, memorable name
	Logo: Stylized bird to the left of the word "ZENEFITS"	Easy-to-recognize logo
	Key brand associations: Streamlined management of employee benefits	Focus on the core value of the offering—employee benefit management

Price	Free	No upfront or recurring costs for using the service
Incentives	None	—
Communication	*Message:* Zenefits simplifies managing employee benefits at no charge	Informs target customers about the company and its services
	Media: Personal sales, press coverage, social media, online advertising, keyword search, zenefits.com website	Broad range of media informs target customers about the company and its services
	Creative format: Simple language delineating the value that Zenefits creates for customers	Direct and to-the-point communication, effective in business-to-business markets
Distribution	Cloud-based service accessible though Zenefits.com website	Easy access from different devices (computer, tablet, phone) and platforms (Windows, Mac, Android)

Zenefits Company Value Map

Company

- **Company profile:** Zenefits is a privately owned software company providing employee benefit solutions to small businesses. The company's core competency is in software development and personal selling.
- **Company goals:** Generate revenues and profits (monetary goal); gain market position, build a strong brand, and create a loyal customer base (strategic goal).

Alternative Options

- **Key alternatives:** Investing in a different business model within the same industry or investing in a different industry.
- **Value proposition of the alternative options:** Potential for higher profits.

Company Value Proposition

- **Company value equation**
  - *Benefits:* Sales revenues and profits (monetary benefits); building a viable company, and creating a loyal customer base (strategic benefits).
  - *Costs:* Research and development costs, service and support expenses, communication costs, sales force costs, general and administrative expenses (monetary costs).
- **Reason to invest:** Potential for exponential market growth and multifold return on investment.

Zenefits Company Offering

Offering	Features	Company value
Product	None	—
Service	[Outlined in the customer value map]	*Benefits:* Developing competency in human resources management *Costs:* R&D and service expenses
Brand	[Outlined in the customer value map]	*Benefits:* Creates brand recognition *Costs:* Brand-building expenses
Price	[Outlined in the customer value map]	*Benefits:* Sales revenue (commissions) *Costs:* None
Incentives	None	—
Communication	[Outlined in the customer value map]	*Benefits:* Informs customers about Zenefits *Costs:* Communication expenses
Distribution	[Outlined in the customer value map]	*Benefits:* Zenefits controls the technological aspects of the cloud-based service *Costs:* Maintaining cloud-based servers, software, user interface, and databases

NOTES

1 Ries, Eric (2011), *The Lean Startup: How Today's Entrepreneurs Use Continuous Innovation to Create Radically Successful Businesses*. New York, NY: Crown Publishing. Blank, Steve and Bob Dorf (2012), *The Startup Owner's Manual: The Step-By-Step Guide for Building a Great Company*. Pescadero, CA: K&S Ranch.

2 Brown, Tim (2008), "Design Thinking," *Harvard Business Review*, 86(6), June 1.

4 The examples used in this chapter are for illustration purposes only and might not adequately reflect the companies' actual positioning strategies.

5 The company-specific information included in the discussion of the business models is presented for illustration purposes only and should not be used on a factual basis.

6 Isaac, Mike and Michael J. de la Merced (2016), "Dollar Shave Club Sells to Unilever for $1 Billion," *New York Times* (July 20). Steele, Anne (2015), "P&G's Gillette Sues Dollar Shave Club," *Wall Street Journal* (December 17).

7 Marquis, Christopher and Laura Velez Villa (2012), *Warby Parker: Vision of a Good Fashion Brand*. Boston, MA: Harvard Business School Publishing. Pressler, Jessica (2013), "20/30 Vision: Warby Parker Has Trained Its Sights on the Stylish, Post-Wealth Millennial Set—As Customers and Employees," *New York* Magazine (August 11).

8 For brevity only the offering for retailers is shown; the offering for contractors and developers follows a similar format.

9 Solomon, Brian (2014), "How Zenefits Beat Out Uber, Airbnb To Become 2014's Hottest Startup," *Forbes* (December 17). Manjoo, Farhad (2014), "Zenefits' Leader Is Rattling an Industry, So Why Is He Stressed Out?," *New York Times* (September 20).

10 Zenefits valuation in 2016 was reduced to $2 billion, in part to account for the company's legal liabilities.

CPSIA information can be obtained
at www.ICGtesting.com
Printed in the USA
LVHW061629170820
663418LV00002B/28

9 781936 572458